Raw is real and no one can live on sugar-coated Christianity. At least that is what my dear friend and fellow seer, Ana Werner, and I both believe. Valleys are a part of the normal Christian life. Part of the problem is, many believers camp out there. But Psalm 23 states, "though I walk through the valley." On the other side of every valley there is another mountain to climb, and when you get to the top of that mountain, your view of everything changes, even the valley you just crawled through. So keep on going. Stretch those muscles of faith and endurance and be a mountain climber. Gain new insight and breathe fresh air by persevering through the various seasons of life to take your promised land! After all, this journey is about gaining an inheritance not just for yourself, but to pioneer for the sake of others. Right? So keep moving forward, knowing all things really do work together for good. Can I get an amen from someone out there?!

JAMES W. GOLL
Founder of God Encounters Ministries
GOLL Ideation LLC
Author, Instructor, Consultant, Recording Artist, and
Communications Coach

Ana Werner meets you where the rubber meets the road. When you read this book, all discouragement will vanish and cause you to dream again!

SID ROTH
Host, *It's Supernatural!*

I love Ana Werner. I love her passion, her love for the Lord and His Word, and her family. She has such a deep faith to believe God, not just for His big promises, but for the "immeasurably more than you could ask or hope for" promises.

In her new book, *Take the Land*, your spirit will be stirred in similar fashion to believe our incredible God for His immeasurably more promises. This book reads like you are sitting down with Ana having coffee as she tells of her power-packed faith journeys. She writes of God's provision and yet, at the same time, life is happening, the family needs dinner, yet each and every paragraph draws you into a deeper faith to believe for greater promises of God.

This book will inspire you to believe and reach for all that God has promised. It will stir up your faith, just like it did mine, to see your promises and to rise up and *Take the Land*.

JULIE MEYER
Author of *30 Days of Praying the Psalms* and *Dreams and Supernatural Encounters*
Intotheriver.net

I remember when I first heard my friend, Ana Werner, share the message that has become this book. There was such anointing and authority in that single statement, *Take the Land*, because it demolishes complacency and summons the people of God to do something with what the Holy Spirit has given them. You don't have to just let life happen to you. You don't need to simply "wait around" until one day, someday, what God said to you just materializes. These are not just words on a page; *Take the Land* is a powerful prophetic call for you to arise and take hold of the promises God has made to you!

LARRY SPARKS

Author of *Pentecostal Fire*

Publisher, Destiny Image

We all know the struggle and reality of "fighting the good fight of faith," "keeping the faith," and as Jesus told Peter, "our faith not failing." These are all necessary to us seeing the promises of God actually manifest in our lives. My friend Ana Werner brings not just insight in her newest book, but also an impartation of faith to not grow weary. Everything we see manifest in the natural is because we have first possessed it in the spiritual. Don't let go. This book will help greatly.

ROBERT HENDERSON

Bestselling Author, *The Courts of Heaven Series*

Ana Werner's book, *Take the Land*, is a timely and insightful analysis of the necessary steps a believer must go through between the new birth and true maturity. The journey that the Christian life takes can be narrow, winding, and steep, but it is also necessary to entering into the fullness of all God's promises. This book will help you to understand how all your experiences and zeal for God fit together for your benefit and His glory.

JOAN HUNTER
Author/Evangelist
TV Host of *Miracles Happen!*

I love this very timely, faith-filled, encouraging, and relatable book reflecting on Ana's spiritual journey and her process of developing faith. By the way, we all go through this. She shares strategies the Lord gave her to endure and overcome. Enjoy this faith-building book and soar!

Jesus asked us in Luke 18:8, *"When I come back, will I find faith on the earth?"*

TRISHA ROSELLE
Founding Co-Pastor, King of Kings Worship Center
Basking Ridge, New Jersey
Author of *21 Day Fast to Break the Cycle of Unbelief*

God told Joshua, concerning the fulfillment of His promise to him and the people of Israel, to be strong and courageous, not to fear anything, and to refuse to be discouraged. God spoke this in the emphatic tense. In other words, God was serious about His covenant with the people but also the land of Israel's inheritance. There is something about land. Land speaks of home, of fruitfulness, and great potential of blessing. Every one of us reading this has a "land of inheritance" that is unique to us and is connected to our destiny. Many times, we can see our "land" but have no idea how to get there or how to possess it! You hold in your hands a manual of breakthrough that not only outlines keys for the journey to the land of promise but how to possess it. Many times, we don't conquer the giants in the "land of promise" because we don't conquer them in our own hearts and lives. Ana addresses all of this and more in an authentic way that will captivate the reader and invite them in a real way into her "journey to promise." As you are inspired by the testimony and the journey Ana has taken, let faith arise that your own journey awaits you and nothing is impossible for those who believe!

BENJAMIN A. DEITRICK
Leader and Visionary, Shekinah Church
Author of *New Breed Arising*

Jesus rent the veil so we can encounter Him in an unending, glorious relationship. But we must open the door. We must risk being known completely, nothing hidden, if we are to be complete in Him. He desires to commune with you, to have relationship with you, and for you to encounter Him in His glory. The more we make room for Him, the more our ability to yield to the Spirit is awakened. Friends, His love is unconditional. You can bring your flaws, failures, and concerns into His presence; and when you are in that face-to-face glory presence, His goodness, loving-kindness, and love will bring you to a point of surrender, peace, cleansing, and forgiveness as you submit yourself to Him. In this place of abiding, it will produce purity, revelation, surrender to His ways, and a life of obedience, a willingness to die to ourselves. Humility is awakened as we remain low in order rise up with a deep work of transformed character formed on the threshing floor of His presence. As we posture ourselves before Him, we know we are not fighting for victory but from victory; and when we are called to wield authority in the Spirit, we are empowered to overcome. In *Take the Land*, my friend Ana has written a raw, transparent, true message that will lead you to a beautiful, authentic, and surrendered relationship with our heavenly Father, Jesus, and Holy Spirit. For all who desire the depth of true intimacy and relationship that has been afforded for each of us, this message is for you. This message opens the doors to deep encounter and personal awakening. Thank you, Ana, for this pure, beautiful, transforming message. You, my friend, are the real deal.

Rebecca Greenwood
Cofounder, Christian Harvest International
Strategic Prayer Apostolic Network
International Freedom Group

Ana offers us an invitation from Heaven. Many of us stand at the precipice of some of our greatest days of victory; just steps away is our promised land! What will we do? Ana Werner's new book, *Take the Land*, is a prophetic reminder of what we have access to in these last days. As we have led revival, Ana personally has been an encouragement to us to not partner with the enemy but to partner with the Holy Spirit to believe for the impossible. I believe that as you read this timely book the gift of faith for your next season will be imparted to you!

JESSI GREEN
Author of *Wildfires*
Director of Saturate Global
JessiGreen.com

This book is perfect for our times. In a season when many believers are on defense and trying to make sense of it all, Ana brings a word from the Holy Spirit that will encourage you to go on offense and see God in His proper light—completely in control and looking for those who would seek His face to bring the Kingdom of Heaven to every facet of their lives. Read *Take the Land* and be encouraged to get in the fight!

PARKER GREEN
Father and disciple-maker

Ephesians 1:11 says, *"In Christ you have obtained an inheritance."* In this book, you will be given keys of knowledge, wisdom, and understanding that will unlock the secrets of how to take your God-given territory! Prepare to receive the inspiration and revelation on how to overcome all things so you can possess what is already yours in Jesus!

APOSTLE TONY KEMP
President of the ACTS GROUP
Tony Kemp Ministries

This is a timely book for those who have found themselves living in discouragement and disappointment that is causing them to give up on the promises God has given them. Ana will share with you from an honest and transparent heart of her own journey of being able to claim her promised land of prophetic promises, dreams, and answered prayers! She will give you practical insight on how to get your confidence back in God so you can pray and contend for your breakthrough!

If you want to be encouraged and strengthened in your faith, then this is the book for you! It's time to take your land!

CAROL KOCH
Founder, Children on the Frontlines
Koch Ministries

Ana has a beautiful way of sharing God's love and expressing her intimate relationship with Him.

In her new book, *Take the Land*, you will be encouraged to look deep into your heart and discover you have the ability to trust God like never before.

You will learn that you can have as much joy and peace before taking the land as after taking the land. We know as you read Ana's testimonies and practical teachings you will be strengthened to remove the hindrances of fear, doubt, and unbelief and enter into the rest of faith. You will make God glad and the devil mad!

Through her compassionate and straightforward way of communicating, Ana will help stir you up to stay in the race, win the race, and obtain the prize of the promise that has been destined for you in Christ Jesus from the foundation of the world!

KEVIN and KATHI ZADAI
Author of *The Agenda of Angels* and
Encountering God's Normal
Warrior Notes Ministry

take the land

DESTINY IMAGE BOOKS BY ANA WERNER

The Seer's Path

Seeing Behind the Veil

Accessing the Greater Glory (with Larry Sparks)

The Warrior's Dance

SELF-PUBLISHED BY ANA WERNER

Letters to the Unforgotten

take the land

IT'S TIME TO STEP INTO YOUR PROMISE FROM GOD

Ana Werner

DESTINY IMAGE® PUBLISHERS, INC.

P.O. Box 310, Shippensburg, PA 17257-0310

"Promoting Inspired Lives."

This book and all other Destiny Image and Destiny Image Fiction books are available at Christian bookstores and distributors worldwide.

For more information on foreign distributors, call 717-532-3040.

Reach us on the Internet: www.destinyimage.com.

ISBN 13 TP: 978-0-7684-5292-1
ISBN 13 eBook: 978-0-7684-6031-5
ISBN 13 HC: 978-0-7684-6033-9
ISBN 13 LP: 978-0-7684-6032-2

For Worldwide Distribution, Printed in the U.S.A.
1 2 3 4 5 6 7 8 / 26 25 24 23 22

Dedication

To all the pioneers, dreamers, visionaries,
and those standing on a promise of God, I
dedicate this book to you.

Keep standing! Don't you quit!

God is faithful.

Acknowledgments

I am so grateful for the steady rock of a husband God gave me in Sam. You have always believed in me, cheered me on, and embraced every adventure God has put us in. As Papa James Goll put it, "He is your anchor to your boat—you are the sail that takes on adventures."

To my amazing children, your childlike faith to just simply believe, "Why wouldn't God just do it?" pushes me daily to grow in my own faith. Watching you add your own chore money to our little jar in the kitchen that says, "All Things Are Possible," as you believe for our "God miracle," makes me so proud of the amazing little people you are growing into.

I want to personally acknowledge and thank our family that continues to stand with us in their faith and prayers through this process. Through the ups and downs, valleys and peaks of this faith walk, you all have cheered us on and helped us in more ways than you may ever know.

To Patricia King, James Goll, and Tony Kemp— thank you all for being champion soundboards, prophetic ears, and a spiritual covering for me and my family. Your covering has been such a blessing for us, and no words can express how grateful I am for all the wisdom and prayers you have sown into my family and ministry.

I am so grateful for my faith-filled friends who stood by us in prayer: Lee and Doris Harms, Becca Greenwood, Julie Meyer, Rick and Lori Taylor, Henry Calcagno, Robert Henderson, Joan Hunter, Larry and Mercedes Sparks, Anthony and Melissa Medina, Jodie and Ben Hughes, Jessi and Parker Green, Ryan Bruss, Kevin and Kathi Zadai, Torrey Marcel Harper, Holly Smith, Krissy Nelson, and Kim Glover.

Sid Roth, I am so grateful for the way you have championed me. I'll never forget the day you leaned over the table and opened the door for me to minister to millions across the world through my own television show. I am blown away over and over by your generosity! I hope to have as much passion and zeal to see the lost come to Jesus all the days of my life.

To my ministry board and team: Melissa Florance, Josiah and Hannah Wyatt, and Kate Ranstrom—you are our forever friends. Yep, you're stuck with us, no matter where we all end up! I'm deeply grateful for all of your friendships and am cheering each one of you on as you pursue all the adventures with God you will go on!

Thank you, Destiny Image team, for all your hard work and energy, helping me put all this together. You guys are amazing and so gracious!

Last, I want to thank those who personally sowed into our vision with their prayers and financial blessings. I pray the Lord blesses you back and that you reap in a great abundance of everything you sowed. May you find your place of peace and deep measures of encounter with the living God!

Contents

Foreword

I celebrate Ana Werner for authoring *Take the Land* and for paying the price that gave her the very authority to write it. In her own walking out of prophetic destiny, she overcame many obstacles and challenges and became aware of valuable keys for breakthrough, which she now uses to encourage and empower others. *Take the Land* is a book that teaches you, the reader, how to engage in your own prophetic journey, embracing the promises and enduring through the testings. Many believers never fulfill their prophetic destiny simply because they lack knowledge of how to partner with the Lord in the journey. It is with this burden that Ana created this treasured resource.

Abraham received prophetic promises from God revealing that he would be a father of nations and that his descendants would be beyond what he could comprehend or count (see Gen. 12:2-3; 13:14-16). What great promises he received, but there actually was nothing in those moments that looked like the promises could possibly come to pass. The promises didn't manifest immediately, and there were obstacles that he had to face and conquer. There were challenges in the natural that would take supernatural intervention to overcome. He was in his older years, his sperm had dried up, and his wife was beyond her child-bearing season. It took great faith to believe that such an extravagant prophetic promise and destiny could possibly be fulfilled. And it would take great patience!

However, Abraham believed and "hoped against hope." He stood on the promises with unwavering commitment and did his best to obey God's leading and instruction. As a result, he eventually enjoyed the fulfillment of all God had promised. Ephesians 3:20 teaches us that, "God is able to do exceedingly abundantly above all we could ask or think." We can see this fulfilled in Abraham's case for sure, but did he walk out his journey perfectly? Not quite! The scripture reveals Abraham's vulnerabilities and "slips" but also how he got back on track. We see his successes and failures in the journey, and we also see God's great grace, mercy, and patience in Abraham's times of struggle. These are helpful and encouraging insights and can be used to help us walk successfully on a path to the fulfillment of our personal prophetic promises.

As a new Christian I received a very powerful prophetic word that revealed my ministry calling. At the time, not one part of the prophecy had been fulfilled. The prophetic word proclaimed things that had never even entered my mind. I wrote out the word from a recording, meditated on the words often, and gave God my, "Be it done unto me according to Your word." Over the following decades, the prophetic word unraveled and came to pass in stages. At the time of this writing almost all of the word has been fulfilled, outside of one declaration that I am confident will come to pass in the next decade or so. As I look back, I can see the journey the Lord led my husband and me on, the obstacles we overcame, and the Spirit-led preparations we walked in to facilitate the fulfillment of the promises. We partnered with the Spirit-infused prophetic declarations and watched them come to pass.

In *Take the Land*, Ana will help you receive your own personal prophetic promises and walk with the Spirit on your own journey unto fulfilled destiny. You will discover important keys that will open doors of understanding, wisdom, and application as you successfully partner with God on this exciting path.

It is your hour to soar and to walk in all the Lord has for you. He is with you as you embark on this exciting adventure. He is stirred with great anticipation and assurance as He dreams of you walking in the fulfillment of your destiny. He is calling you onward and upward. Are you ready? If so, then take His hand and follow Him as He leads you into the fullness of what you were created for! Move forward with confidence and "take the land."

PATRICIA KING

Introduction

Today marks a fresh start for you. I pray that, as you take this book up in your hands and daily read the words that fall upon the page, you feel the Holy Spirit pour into you. May you be encouraged with strength, boldness, and courage to believe that the promise of God over your life is yes and amen! May your vision be restored, and may God bring clarity to where He is leading you.

I don't know where your journey of faith has taken you. You may find yourself now, as I do, in years of praying and contending for the "B" word. Breakthrough is the word I'm going for here! Or maybe you're just starting your journey of believing in faith for something. Wherever you are in the process of walking into the promised land of God for your life, I know that God wants to encourage you today.

Keep going! Don't you quit believing and trusting in God!

Let's begin our walk of faith together. I want you to know that I have prayed for each person whose eyes fall on these pages—that the impartation of faith, endurance, and strength would fall upon you.

Your Enemy

I am absolutely convinced that in this hour the Lord's eyes are skimming the earth, looking to find a people who are full of faith, full of adoration for Him, and who are unwavering in the presence of our enemies.

Perhaps today your greatest enemy is self-doubt. Or perhaps your greatest enemy could be fear itself. Often, our natural tendencies are to make the devil and his schemes way bigger than our God. Do you know what it says in the Word?

"The God of peace will soon crush Satan under your feet" (Rom. 16:20). It also says: "You prepare a table before me in the presence of my enemies" (Ps. 23:5).

Let me start off by reminding you today, or giving you a small meditative point to ponder—God is so much bigger than the devil! I know you already know this and have heard this, especially if you have been a believer for any amount of time. But do you really believe it? Jesus defeated him on the cross and on that we can stand in confidence.

It's time to get your confidence in God back!

Although when warfare comes—and sometimes it pours—it sure does remain hard to stand in "confidence."

IT'S TIME TO GET YOUR CONFIDENCE IN GOD BACK!

A Reminder

I remember one day specifically when the Lord radically changed my mindset about the way I was seeing the devil. I had a deadline put on me from the Holy Spirit to complete a book, as well as the daily ins and outs of parenting. At the time, my husband and I had taken on a daring project of renovating a 1930s house. And when I say renovating, I don't mean just a small task of making a few changes. No, no! I'm talking about a gut job of ripping out everything and literally starting with the bones of the home.

So I found myself in the midst of a demolition site, dust all around, a hole in our dining room peering straight up into the bathroom upstairs, trying to find a peaceful and clean place to sit and write. In that moment, the warfare to even begin to write felt almost too much to handle.

"God, I am so overwhelmed! I just can't do this!" was my inward cry.

To my surprise, I heard back a clear reply from the Lord: "You are only as overwhelmed as you make it. Whose voice are you agreeing with right now? I'm much bigger than all of this."

It was a simple reminder, but that reminder has stuck with me all my days. I was reminded that day that our God is bigger than any attack and weapons of warfare I may ever experience. He is in control, and He is peace. The enemy is always trying to steal our peace. Here's the thing though. It's hard for our minds to wrap around it, but Jesus, being fully man and fully God, didn't just desire peace—He was and is peace.

The more I have meditated on this aspect of Jesus' nature, the less I become so reactive to the enemy's plots and schemes to take me out.

Peace I leave you, My peace I give you; not as the world gives, do I give to you. Do not let your hearts be troubled, nor fearful (John 14:27).

So before we begin, I want to ask you to stop and ponder over a few points.

Be honest; this is between you and the Holy Spirit. Know that I am asking myself the same questions to ponder over with you. Do yourself a favor and take time to actually pray through them. Don't just skim the questions, like most of us do when we see questions in books! Answering these questions will actually help you.

1. Is there any area of my life where I am actually being reactive to the enemy right now?

2. What lies have I come into agreement with that are not of God?

3. Now let's ask Holy Spirit, what is the actual truth?

CHAPTER 1

You Were Destined to Reign

I am 100 percent convinced that this season we are in right now is the time to take land back from the enemy. The enemy of this world is on the prowl, and he is conniving in character. The devil wants nothing more than to stop you right now from pushing forward and taking back what is rightfully yours.

You have a destiny! Your destiny is so much bigger and better than you can even imagine. Did you know that Heaven is cheering you on?

Therefore, since we also have such a great cloud of witnesses surrounding us, let's rid ourselves of every obstacle and the sin which so easily entangles us, and let's run with endurance the race that is set before us, looking only at Jesus, the originator and perfecter of the faith, who for the joy set before Him endured the cross, despising the shame, and has sat down at the right hand of the throne of God (Hebrews 12:1-2).

You know how Holy Spirit highlights certain parts of a passage to catch your attention? Two things about this scripture jump out to me. First, the mention of the cloud of witnesses that surround us. Heaven is looking in. Did you know that?

Once, my spiritual eyes were opened to actually see this. I'll never forget it. I was filming my television show, *Eagles Arise,* for Sid Roth. Apostle Tony Kemp was my guest on the show and we were talking about the glory of God. The cameras were rolling, all eyes fixed on us, and suddenly my eyes were opened.

Open visions are interesting and often hard to explain. The best way I can describe an open vision is like a film rolling or transposed over the natural. As we sat there, I suddenly saw all these people from Heaven looking into the room. Hundreds of them sat pressing in to see what was going on. Their faces were full of joy and they were cheering us on.

Now before you set this book down and think I've totally lost it here, I want to challenge you. What if, just maybe, I haven't! John writes about an open vision in the book of Revelation in the Bible.

> *After these things I looked, and behold, a door standing open in heaven, and the first voice which I had heard, like the sound of a trumpet speaking with me, said, "Come up here"* (Revelation 4:1).

Personally, I'll never forget that moment in the studio. Time stood still as I realized that Heaven is watching and cheering us on. Suddenly, Heaven seemed all the closer. The whole notion of having a "heavenly perspective" became all the more real, and boy, did my perspective shift.

WHEN WE GET OUR MINDS RENEWED AND TRANSFORMED BY THE REALITY OF HEAVEN, PRIORITIES GET SHIFTED.

In the timeline of God, you and I have a small window to make a difference in this planet. When we get our minds renewed and transformed by the reality of Heaven, priorities get shifted. Suddenly, the things that seemed to bother us or drive our ambitions get changed. When we get Heaven on our mind and He melts our heart to match His, suddenly we find purpose.

Let me share with you another vision. Nothing like starting off a book by sharing nuggets from encounters with Heaven!

Once I was taken up into a vision. I walked into a room where before my eyes I could see many seats lining the room. Immediately, I could discern the importance of the room. This was a place where decisions were made! This was a place of meeting with purpose. Jesus suddenly appeared in the room. He was dressed with robes that were thick and royal purple.

"The Governmental Room," He spoke to me. "Ana, it's time to take your seat."

He motioned to a chair along the wall and smiled encouragingly at me.

I struggled and wrestled with approaching the chair. In my mind, I battled with my thoughts. *Surely there are people more deserving to sit in a governmental seat like this, who have far greater accomplishments that I do,* I thought.

Knowing my thoughts, He repeated, "It's time to take your seat."

I sat down in the chair, and with my eyes closed something wild took place. (As if this could get any wilder!) With my eyes closed, I suddenly saw hundreds and thousands of faces of people one by one before me, and I just knew these were the faces of the people I would pour into. These were the faces of people God was giving me His heart for. One by one, I kept seeing them.

"It will cost you to sit here, but it's time," He spoke.

That phrase has forever been imprinted in me. I've revisited those words several times as I ponder over them. You and I were destined to reign:

> *We have become his poetry, a re-created people that will fulfill the destiny he has given each of us, for we are joined to Jesus, the Anointed One. Even before we were born, God planned in advance our destiny and the good works we would do to fulfill it!* (Ephesians 2:10 TPT)

But that word reign actually looks different from Heaven's perspective. Jesus reigns, and He poured out everything. He shed blood so that we might reign with Him. Scripture says He was unrecognizable for what He endured on the cross.

It's important to stop and remember just what He went through for you and me, for the sake of love. Loving Him fully means allowing Him to transform our mind. To reign with Him, you and I must have a heavenly transformed mind—the mind of Christ.

> *Be inwardly transformed by the Holy Spirit through a total reformation of how you think.*

This will empower you to discern God's will as you live a beautiful life, satisfying and perfect in his eyes (Romans 12:2 TPT).

What's on Christ's mind is people. So sitting on my governmental seat in Heaven that day meant so much more than just the idea, "I was created to reign." The soberness of the moment hit me strongly. The responsibility that Christ was showing me—I can't even put it into words. Heaven's perspective is the only way I know how to put it.

You and I were created to reveal His kingdom to the world. And do you know what? The world is hurting right now! If we just stop and look, people all around us are hurt and disappointed with what life's handed them. The enemy of this world does everything he can to rob and destroy the wonderful plans and purposes of the Lord.

People need to know the hope of Jesus. They need to know the hope of Jesus through you!

Perhaps right now you find yourself in the place where you need to feel and know hope again. Do you know God has a purpose for your life?

But the Lord's plans stand firm forever; his intentions can never be shaken (Psalm 33:11 NLT).

God has a plan.

You may not be able to see it right now, but do me a favor. Actually, do yourself a favor, and begin to hope again. God's got great, great things in store for your life.

You and I were given a small window on God's time-line to impact this world. So what are you going to do with it? Who has God placed in your life, right in front of you, whom you can impact? Often the enemy will use the comparison game to get us to feel inadequate or not important enough to really impact the world. We can fall into the mental trap of, "Well, I'm not doing that much that's important. I'm just at home here with my kids every day making lunches for school!" Or, "I'm not impacting the world, I'm just a fitness instructor."

You fill in your own "I'm just" blank, but I'll tell you something again: Heaven's cheering you on! Each person you and I come into contact with is an opportunity for us to be Jesus to them. You and I are His ambassadors. This earth isn't our permanent home, but just a temporary one.

HEAVEN'S CHEERING YOU ON!

With that in mind, how can you live on purpose? What is God asking you to do today? Perhaps it's simply calling someone or sending a text to a friend who's going through a rough season, just to remind them how Christ sees them. Don't underestimate the power of a kind word!

Let's dive back into that scripture.

> *Therefore, since we also have such a great cloud of witnesses surrounding us, let's rid ourselves of every obstacle and the sin which so easily entangles us, and let's run with endurance the race that is set before us, looking only at Jesus, the originator and perfecter of the faith, who for the joy set before Him endured the cross, despising the shame, and has sat down at the right hand of the throne of God* (Hebrews 12: 1-2).

When we get a transformed or renewed mind and begin to see things from Heaven's perspective, I believe it will change even the way we view the promises of God for our lives.

I believe that each one of us has a plan and a promise of God over our lives. God's given everyone a purpose. Even from the very beginning of time, Adam and Eve had a purpose!

> *Then the Lord God took the man and put him in the Garden of Eden to cultivate it and tend it* (Genesis 2:15).

You have a promise and a purpose from God. Even though it may have seemed like it's been sitting on a shelf for a while now, collecting dust, I want to remind you that God has not forgotten.

To fulfill that promise—you know, that promise that you have been contending over for a while now—this scripture points us to a key. Fix your eyes on Jesus! This is a season in which many have been waiting for a promise of God to be fulfilled. We have been praying for years and standing in faith for that thing to come about, fighting off discouragement, fighting off doubt, fighting back tears while we wait. Now is the time!

It's time to take the land. It's time to walk into your promise of God. The timeline of Jesus' return is ticking, and I believe this is a season when it's all hands on deck. We are in an accelerated season of the Lord. We are walking in destiny and purpose because He is calling the lost home. He is setting everything in motion. This is the time of the greatest harvest of souls we have yet to see, and for that reason God needs you to be walking in your destiny! He needs you to be fulfilling your purpose—because you are a part of His timeline! How great is that, when you really sit back and think about it! You and I—our little lives are a part of a much greater story that gives us purpose. We are on His timeline! Joshua 1:2-3,6 says:

> *Moses My servant is dead; so now arise, cross this Jordan, you and all this people, to the land which I am giving to them, to the sons of Israel. Every place on which the sole of your foot*

steps, I have given it to you. ...Be strong and courageous.

Moses had just passed away, and now it was up to Joshua to lead the Israelites into the Promised Land. This land had been promised to them for years. Let's follow this story all the way back to Moses' encounter with the burning bush found in Exodus 3. I'll pick out the highlights, but please go read the entire chapter for yourself.

> *Now Moses was pasturing the flock of his father-in-law Jethro, the priest of Midian; and he led the flock to the west side of the wilderness and came to Horeb, the mountain of God. Then the angel of the Lord appeared to him in a blazing fire from the midst of a bush* (Exodus 3:1-2).

> *"Moses, Moses!" And he said, "Here I am." Then He said, "Do not come near here; remove your sandals from your feet, for the place on which you are standing is holy ground"* (Exodus 3:4-5).

> *I have certainly seen the oppression of My people who are in Egypt.... So I have come down to rescue them from the power of the Egyptians, and to bring them up from that land to a good and spacious land, to a land flowing with milk and honey* (Exodus 3:7-8).

Forty years! Forty years the Israelites carried this promise as they wandered through the desert—someday they would enter into the Promised Land. (You can find the reference to 40 years in Numbers 14:33.)

Forty years is a long time! Can you imagine the state in which Joshua and the Israelites must have found themselves? Their leader Moses had now passed away at 120 years of age; they'd been wandering around and around for 40 years, and now God charged them to step in and take the land!

It brings tears to my eyes as I think that perhaps you can relate to this story. (I can too!) Perhaps it's been years of waiting, hoping, and thinking that that promise is finally coming. After some time passes, let's be real—it gets harder and harder to stand in that "childlike faith" and just believe.

And then God gives a charge: Arise! Cross over! Now is the time.

ARISE! CROSS OVER! NOW IS THE TIME.

So—if you are willing—gear yourself back up, look at the mountain that might be standing in front of you, and declare with me, "Now is the time! Now is the time for me to step in and claim the promise that God has for me!"

Let's advance together. It's time to believe again.

CHAPTER 2

In the Waiting

My deep need calls out to the deep kindness of your love. Your waterfall of weeping sent waves of sorrow over my soul, carrying me away, cascading over me like a thundering cataract.

Yet all day long God's promises of love pour over me. Through the night I sing his songs, for my prayer to God has become my life.

I will say to God, "You are my mountain of strength; how could you forget me? Why must I suffer this vile oppression of my enemies—these heartless tormentors who are out to kill me?"

Their wounding words pierce my heart over and over while they say, "Where is this God of yours?"

So I say to my soul, "Don't be discouraged. Don't be disturbed. For I know my God will break through for me." Then I'll have plenty of reasons to praise him all over again. Yes, living before his face is my saving grace! (Psalm 42:7-11 TPT)

Living Before His Face Is My Saving Grace!

You know, let's be honest. I don't know what it is about our culture, but when we see scriptures posted in Christian books, our natural tendency is to just skim it or even read past it. However, this scripture is so powerful!

When the need runs deep, and when you find yourself in that place of tears in the process of waiting for the promise to come, when you feel like you are suffocating in discouragement—then He comes. His love pours over us and becomes a healing balm for our souls. It's a tender place, and He draws near.

One day very recently, I was crying out to God and my best friend on earth—my mom. Being extremely prophetically wired, the two of us were both reminiscing how the day before had been such a day of momentum, moving forward to a promise of God I personally have been contending over for a few years now. I knew and could feel we were one step closer. Then the next morning I woke up, and bam—discouragement and a mountain of impossibilities were thrown back in my face.

This pattern I have learned to recognize as a very sneaky strategy from the enemy. Although it's predictable, for whatever reason it never ceases to surprise me. Right before breakthrough comes a bit of warfare, and then directly after a promotion also comes a bit of warfare, nipping at the heels.

Can I get an amen here? Can you relate at all?

You get a phone call, perhaps one that you have been awaiting for a long time now. A relationship seems to be restored, or at least it's a start. Then right on the heels of that phone call comes disappointment or a letdown.

Why does it come?

THE ENEMY IS ABSOLUTELY AFRAID OF YOU MAKING PROGRESS FORWARD.

Let me share with you. The enemy is absolutely afraid of you making progress forward. One more step forward means a retreat for him, and so the warfare comes. Don't worry, this entire book is not about the enemy, but I do believe that by seeing his strategies we won't be so ambushed and can learn to recognize his foolish ways.

If you are disappointed right now or can relate, I want you to do me a favor. Take a moment and literally laugh. Laugh out loud right now, even if you don't feel like it. Do it, and laugh at the enemy.

Your progress is actually frustrating him. So often in the heat of the moment, we place ourselves as the victims of his attacks. But honestly, the devil is on the retreat.

Back to my story. So as Mom and I were sitting there, seeing the pattern of the enemy's attack, in my frustration I cried out, "It's not that I don't see the pattern. I see it and I recognize this setback today is just the enemy trying to hit me with discouragement. But here's the thing. It's not that I don't see the battle. It's that I'm sick of the battle! I want this pattern to stop! If Moses cried out to God and was able to change God's mind, shouldn't I be able to cry out to God in my frustration? I'm contending, I'm standing in faith, I'm not wavering in my belief in the impossible. But here's the thing. I need God to come through now! I'm putting this on Him to come through for me."

The silence hung in the air for a few seconds between the two of us. I myself couldn't even believe what I had just said. It was a raw moment. I had allowed someone this close into the very depths of my heart's cry. I had laid it out in that vulnerable place, and there it seemed to hang. My mom, being the amazing encourager and intercessor that she is, blessed me with her kind words as we said our goodbyes and hung up.

The words still hung in the air. I could feel the tension of feeling almost ashamed of the very place my heart was at, and yet Holy Spirit's presence was tangibly filling my car.

"God?" I asked.

"I'm here," I heard in response.

Just a phrase. That was it. But that phrase was all I needed, actually.

"I'm here."

It wasn't an answer to the questions that lingered— the hows and whys and whens in my heart that would still be left to be answered. Believe it or not, though, the "I'm here" was actually the comfort I needed.

Good old Webster's dictionary defines isolation as the complete separation of others.

I have noticed this pattern—when the warfare seems heavy, we often can feel pretty isolated or far from God. "Where are You, God?" seems to be the cry of our hearts. It's like as warfare increases, in our misunderstanding we think that God decreases. We feel alone in the battle and abandoned by our heavenly Father.

"I hear You," I responded to the voice I heard. "All I know to do right now is to run to You. Here I am. I'm feeling broken. I'm feeling weak. I know I'm not, but I feel so weak in this moment. I know this discouragement will pass, but in this moment, God, I need You," I cried out to Him.

"I'm here," I heard again.

"God, I'm frustrated. We keep taking steps of faith, getting prophetic words, and believing in the promises—and yet here we meet again. I still feel stuck in the same place, feeling like I still don't have it all together. Process isn't my favorite thing, Lord, You know that. I want answers. I want clarity. Have I missed it? Is my timing off? I thought I heard You, Lord, but now I'm so confused. Why can't I see You as I see for others so clearly?"

"I'm right here. Come to Me. Let Me strengthen you."

I know. I know as you are reading this right now that this may not seem to you like the most encouraging Father. He didn't answer my raw moment in the way I wanted Him to answer. He gave me what I needed the most. I mean, here I am a ministry leader, but I was feeling weaker than ever in my own faith.

My eyes hurt from crying hard. Honestly, sometimes we need to have a good cry out with God. It can be the most healing thing for our souls. In that raw place—you know, that place you don't show anyone—He meets you. I hope it encourages you as you read this. You aren't the only one who struggles sometimes with discouragement and the waiting process!

Let me encourage you—you are going to get through this. You will see the other side. Years from now, you may look back on this very season and see how God's hand was in it all—the timing, the going through the fire experiences, the testing of your faith, the plans. He doesn't desire for you to be stuck, no matter how stuck you may feel right now. You're crossing over.

YOU'RE CROSSING OVER.

Let's take a moment, before moving on too quickly, to get raw with God. Go ahead; lay it all out there. Remember that moment for the disciples.

> *Jesus, knowing that the Father had given all things into His hands, and that He had come from God and was going to God, rose from supper and laid aside His garments, took a towel and girded Himself. After that, He poured water into a basin and began to wash the disciples' feet, and to wipe them with the towel with which He was girded* (John 13:3-5 NKJV).

Knowing He was on the way to the cross and these were the last precious moments He had before His resurrection, Jesus got down and washed their dirty feet.

That's your Jesus! He's not afraid of messy!

Our emotions, our places of pain, our places of discouragement or frustration aren't too much for Him to take. He already did take it all, in fact, on that cross. Jesus experienced the very thing you are feeling right now.

It's time to get real with Him. I don't know about you, but sometimes we just need to lay aside our religious ways of entering into His Presence. I want to encourage you to just be still. Invite the Holy Spirit into this very moment and ask Holy Spirit to examine your heart.

Heart check—how's your heart really doing in this moment?

Some of us like to stuff things so far down that we may not even know how to answer that. Honestly, pause and ask yourself—how's my heart doing today?

Pause and wait for an answer to that question, just between you and the Lord. Holy Spirit will show you. What He shows you might actually surprise you. He did for me the other day. In that raw moment of frustration, He came in the tenderest way. I brought my fleshly heart to Him, hurting, frustrated, and discouraged. In a vision, I watched as He held it tenderly and cared for it.

I dare you to pour out everything at His feet right now. This is your moment! I know it doesn't feel like it, but this is a moment of real breakthrough. It's here in this messy place that our hearts reconnect to the Father's through the process of waiting for our promise.

I call this place the threshing floor.

When my husband and I were missionaries in Nepal, we got to witness the process of how rice is actually made. You know rice—that staple grain that nearly half the world's population survives off of. Those little grains that we so easily purchase in the grocery store here in the States. Man, do we take for granted the process of the labor someone actually went through to make that little grain!

With an old sickle in our hands, we helped cut the grass that carried the grains. Then we watched as the native Nepalese showed us how to separate the grains from the husks. (They did it with such ease and skill!)

Then there was a further process, and this was the one that the Holy Spirit used to minister to me. I watched as the grains, which still had their thick, tough shells on, were pressed through a metal rolling machine that crushed the grains and spit out the rice kernels onto a floor. Thousands of rice kernels shot out everywhere. While everyone was getting wildly excited, there I found myself with tears welling up.

Holy Spirit was speaking.

The concept of "and this is what our walk feels like sometimes" hit me. We all go through those seasons of pressing, dying to our own self, and out of those experiences pops the beautiful fruit of character, steady faith, and worship that doesn't quit.

> ## OUT OF THOSE EXPERIENCES POPS THE BEAUTIFUL FRUIT OF CHARACTER, STEADY FAITH, AND WORSHIP THAT DOESN'T QUIT.

May I remind you again—Jesus is not afraid of messes. We can put Him in a box, or think we have to have it all together with our life looking perfectly polished, and yet we are so wrong.

Relationship looks like freedom from fear. Freedom to run right up to the throne, arms wide open, yelling, "Here I am, Daddy!"

> *So now we draw near freely and boldly to where grace is enthroned, to receive mercy's kiss and discover the grace we urgently need to strengthen us in our time of weakness* (Hebrews 4:16 TPT).

Freedom looks like dancing widely in passionate love, not caring what anyone thinks.

> *And David was dancing before the Lord with all his strength, and David was wearing a linen ephod. So David and all the house of Israel were bringing up the ark of the Lord with joyful shouting and the sound of the trumpet* (2 Samuel 6:14-15).

Freedom looks like running forward like a stallion bursting into that open field, just for the sake of not missing your moment to run with Jesus.

> *I don't know about you, but I'm running hard for the finish line. I'm giving it everything I've got* (1 Corinthians 9:26 MSG).

Relationship looks like looking up through eyes full of tears and saying, "Here I am, Jesus. Here's all of me, and yet You still love me and pick me up."

> *Move your heart closer and closer to God, and he will come even closer to you. But make sure you cleanse your life* (James 4:8 TPT).

It's time. This is your moment.

Come to Him. Meet Him at that threshing floor in whatever state of disbelief you may find yourself in, and bring Him your heart.

You aren't too much for Him. And your promise still remains.

This is the starting place of crossing over.

The threshing floor is the starting place.

CHAPTER 3

Fixed Focus

*Do not turn from it to the right or to the left,
so that you may achieve success wherever you go
(Joshua 1:7).*

Can I be brutally honest with you here? It's not enough
to have a promise from God. To walk into that promise
there are a few key ingredients that need to be applied,
and one of those is a fixed focus.

In this scripture, a hidden treasure found in the
book of Joshua, God commanded the Israelites to keep

their eyes fixed and focused straight ahead. You know why, don't you? God knew there tend to be distractions when we are close to a promise.

Let's look at the history of the Israelites. God let them out of Egypt through Moses parting the Red Sea. As Moses went up onto Mount Sinai into the very Presence to inquire of the Lord and receive the Ten Commandments, we see the Israelites waiting down below—building false idols.

The Lord had strictly given Moses the command-ment "You shall have no other gods before Me" (Exod. 20:3), but in the delay of Moses coming down the mountain, the Israelites compromised.

In the delay they compromised!

IN THE DELAY THEY COMPROMISED!

So it makes sense later for the Lord to challenge them to have a fixed focus, not looking to the right or to the left.

The Birthing Room

I remember when I had my son, the labor was very dif-ferent from my daughter. We had waited a little too long at home, and barely made it to the hospital. Upon arrival, I was already at a 9 dilated (and 10 is go-time).

My midwife wasn't there yet. She got the call and was frantically racing to make it to the hospital on time.

You know, you can have your peaceful birthing plan all laid out, and then nothing seems to go as planned! (Hopefully for you, if you're an expectant momma reading this, that won't be the case, but each time that's how it's rolled for me.)

The goal is to maintain your peace and breathe in the midst of what feels like chaos. Teams of bustling nurses and doctors, machines, and bright lights all swarmed me. Hardly anything like my birth plan of a few people, a quiet room, and low lighting to help me ease into pushing this human out of my body! They bustled, and the pain intensified. My husband tried his best to protect me from the chaos and help me keep my peace.

Just breathe—or scream at everyone—just breathe.

Like an angel descending from Heaven, my midwife showed up, not even scrubbed up yet, but in her jeans and a hoodie. She took one look at the situation and took command.

"Everyone get out of here! I want just one nurse and her husband to be in here. Dim those lights, turn off that racket, move those machines away. Get me a warm towel," she hollered.

I sighed in relief!

She got right up in my face.

"Okay hon. I need you to focus now. Forget about everything else. Don't worry about anyone else. You've got a job to do. If you want to deliver this baby, he'll be out here within twenty minutes. But I need you to focus now," she strongly encouraged me.

Then Sam, my husband, grabbed my hand and held it hard. "You've got this! You can do this!" he cheered me on.

Those two, my husband and my midwife, gave me the encouragement and direction I needed, and literally within 20 minutes our roaring son was born.

I have reflected back on that experience many times.

With each staff member bustling about, each machine beeping at me, inwardly I tightened up. I couldn't focus and was distracted by all the swirls around me. They delayed the process.

Just when I felt like giving up and I couldn't go on any longer, God sent those two angels to clear the atmosphere and give direction.

TOO MANY PEOPLE IN THE BIRTHING ROOM CAN DELAY THE PROCESS.

When you are contending to take the land or walking into a promise of God over your life, having too many people in the birthing room can delay the process.

Birthing Forth

Right now as you are reading this, a shift is coming. You are close now, so it's time to narrow your focus. You are birthing part of your destiny, part of generations to come after you as well. So please take your promise more seriously! It's an assignment of the Lord.

Personally, as I am writing this my husband and I are also contending for something in faith, so I'm right there with you in that place of contending. Very early on with this current promise, the Lord showed me what happened at my son's birth and reminded me, "Be careful whom you allow into the birthing room."

BE CAREFUL WHOM YOU ALLOW INTO THE BIRTHING ROOM.

I've learned from previous mistakes in the past to not rush forward and, like a gushing spring, share with the world, "I'm taking this step of faith!" Because, let me tell you, with great measures or leaps of faith comes much pushback from the enemy and many chances for discouragement.

Confusion and Delay, the Outside Concerned Voices

I remember when I heard a clear word from the Lord to write my first book, and that I was called to birth the ministry. I was pregnant at the time with my firstborn. I shared with many people the promise, full of joy and expectation for them to be joyous with me!

Boy, was I in for a surprise.

Day by day God would say, "Take this step of faith," and then directly following the voice of God, the phone calls and texts started pouring in.

"I'm concerned for the welfare of your children. Don't they need a mother at home? How will you manage being a mother, and also caring for others? Are you choosing ministry over your family? How could you do that? I'm concerned for your marriage. This could put a wedge between you and Sam. Some men aren't able to handle having their wife being in the limelight."

I would hang up the phone, thanking them for their concern. I would delete the texts frantically so I wouldn't be tempted to re-read them. But you know what happened, don't you? I took the poison. I took the enemy's bait. The enemy would speak through these whispers of concern and mess with my head. I'd lie awake at night crying out to God.

"God, why are You having me birth a ministry now? Why couldn't we birth this after we've had children? I don't see many moms my age doing full-time ministry and being a mom. Is this even possible? Can't it wait until our children are full grown and out of the house?

And what about my marriage? How will it be for Sam if he's back at home with the kids and I'm out doing a TV show or an interview? Will he feel frustrated or angry at being stuck at home? Will he resent me or the ministry call You've put on my life? I know I've heard You, but now I'm so confused!"

"So confused" was exactly what happened. I would be awake wrestling under this confusion for days upon days, all while trying to take care of the growing human inside of me and write my first book.

I still pushed through and wrote that book, but I can tell you honestly that the process was more painful than it could have been. I had to contend for my peace to birth the ministry. There were days I would wake up and feel like I just wanted to quit. I hope it's okay I'm being real with you here. Ministry is not always glamorous. In reality, it's more about death to self daily and Him being glorified through you and through the process.

> ## IT'S ABOUT DEATH TO SELF DAILY AND HIM BEING GLORIFIED THROUGH YOU.

As you take steps of faith, watch for the enemy to hit you with discouragement and confusion directly after taking that step. You must be doing something right if you are making him move on the defense!

There's a scripture in Ephesians that says we do not wrestle against flesh and blood, but against principalities (see Eph. 6:12). That scripture became more real for me than ever before. I would see the direct correlation between hearing a promise, taking a leap of faith, and then directly after being hit with a word of discouragement.

There's a pattern.

Their concerns were valid. But did I need to hear them in that moment of birthing a promise? No!

You are in a time right now of birthing, I have no doubt. Otherwise you wouldn't have picked up this book in the first place. You are pressing and contending for what God has showed you. It won't be easy. It will take immense faith.

Sound Counsel

Looking back on what I walked through with the completion of my first book, I learned to be more careful who I allow into the birthing process. All the other voices of opinion, despite their good intentions, the enemy can use to delay the process and bring on confusion.

You need sound counsel surrounding you. You need people like my husband and midwife were in that birthing room—those who can nudge you, redirect you, speak into you words of faith when you can't hear correctly. You need people cheering you on when you feel like quitting.

It's good to have solid wisdom and counsel. I surround myself with people who can speak into my life, even if it's with words of correction. We all need correction. We need people who won't just agree but will really hear God and speak into us. Those handful of people are faith filled! Their words, even if they carry correction, are still full of faith and hope.

Did you know that faith is the opposite of fear? You don't need fear and discouragement shouting at you right now. Not when you are this close to birthing something big with God. You are close. It's time to get serious.

Different This Time

This time, I find myself in a different place. I'm believing in God for something much larger than I could ever do myself. He's stretching my faith in every way possible. He's challenging me in new places that I need to be challenged in. Mind you, I have huge child-like faith. I believe His word. I believe God can do the impossible. I believe in His miracles and have witnessed countless miracles around the world for others.

It's always easier to believe for others than to believe for our own promises though, right?

So this time, it's different. Along this journey of contending for something in faith right now, God said to me, "Be careful who you allow in the birthing place." So I prayed. In my zealousness, I'm not shouting from the rooftops this exciting promise God has shown me. Mind you, when this promise comes true, what a wonderful testimony it will be of His incredible faithfulness. I can't wait to share it with everyone. That will have to wait, though. I'm in the birthing process, so I have to stay focused.

I prayed and shared with a handful of faith-filled friends. Friends who have faith to see beyond the limitations that are screaming at my face. Friends I know will not speak discouragement or doubts.

Moses had Aaron and Hur hold up his arms in a time of war. I often think of that when I am being stretched in new areas of faith. If Moses needed friends like that, I think we do too (see Exod. 17:12).

Who is in your birthing room right now? I want to advise you to reconsider your counsel. Who will hold up your arms, who will hold up your faith in this time of birthing destiny? You don't need everyone speaking into the situation.

You may even need to narrow down who you are listening to in order to keep your focus. You may need to stop, pause, and ask Holy Spirit who is bringing confusion by speaking into your vision right now. You may even feel challenged to put stronger boundaries down or limit interactions with those influencers for a season.

May the Lord bring forth the right people and bring clarity right now to any confusion you have been under recently. I pray that the whispers of discouragement from the enemy would be silenced in the name of Jesus. May you now be infiltrated with faith to rise back up, even if you find yourself on the ground in this very moment, with very little strength to go on pursuing the dream. May clarity return.

That's right. It's time to rise back up.

God has known your destiny from the very moment you were just a thought in His mind. Despite the setback you may have walked through, He has always known you can do this! He's calling you to rise up to a new level of faith.

HE HAS ALWAYS KNOWN YOU CAN DO THIS!

Distractions Go in Jesus' Name!

I find the story of Nehemiah's rebuilding of the wall an interesting one to ponder. In case you have never read the story, I'm going to summarize a portion of scripture for you.

The walls of Jerusalem had been broken down, and its gates were burnt as well. Back then, the walls and gates of a city were very important. It is what would fortify the city and its people within from the attacks of its enemies.

Nehemiah was devastated at hearing about the broken state Jerusalem was in.

Sometimes God births something amazing by giving you a burden for something first. Nehemiah was given the burden and direction from the Lord to rebuild the wall of the city.

Let's pick up in Nehemiah 6.

Nehemiah wrote, "I had rebuilt the wall, and that no breach was left in it, although at that time I had not installed the doors in the gates" (Neh. 6:1).

So it was not totally secure yet. Remember the birthing metaphor. This would be "go time." He had almost done it, just not quite finished securing the city. Wouldn't it be like the enemy to come now with distractions to throw him off course?

When you are close to birthing a promise, it's time to narrow that focus and say no to distractions!

Two enemies of Nehemiah attempted to lure him off the project and off the wall. They said, "Come, let's meet together at Chephirim in the plain of Ono [one of the other villages]" (Neh. 6:2).

But Nehemiah had wisdom to recognize they were planning to harm him. Look at his response!

> *I am doing a great work and am unable to come down. Why should the work stop while I leave it and come down to you?* (Nehemiah 6:3)

This perhaps is one of my favorite scriptures in the Bible. Five times they tried to pull Nehemiah off his assignment from the Lord, but he recognized the enemy's hand in all of it.

> *For all of them were trying to frighten us, thinking, "They will become discouraged with the work and it will not be done." But now, God, strengthen my hands* (Nehemiah 6:9).

First off, when God calls you and me to do something, we have to take it seriously. You are doing a great work and cannot afford to be distracted right now.

It's time to narrow your focus.

Narrowing your focus may mean saying no to not only other people's voices, but also saying no to other needs that may come to distract. It's not that you won't pick them back up later; it's just that this isn't your season to juggle it all.

This will now be my sixth book I've written. Every time I get a word from the Lord to write a book, I have to adjust my schedule. Together as a family we look at our schedules and see how we can carve out time and lessen my load so that I can focus, press in, and birth a book. (All authors reading this understand what I mean. Writing a novel is like birthing a baby, in a way.)

Suddenly, when God gives you a new assignment, you will find yourself with every temptation to be distracted staring you in the face. Pulled in many directions, you may find yourself wondering, *How I will ever juggle it all and yet do this thing God is asking me to do?*

Just say no.

Yep, you heard me. Just say no to other or extra demands. Literally, this has been one of the best tips of advice a friend has ever given me.

It may not be a forever no—it may be more like a "just not right now." If Nehemiah did it, so can you!

Tips to Narrowing Down

In my own life, I have some simple examples of narrowing my focus and saying no:

1. Turning off my phone, computer, and all screen devices

2. Learning to not overcommit myself

3. Setting reasonable goals

4. Finding a quiet space to dream with God

5. Saying no to commitments (even ones that seem great but will suck my time and energy)

6. Releasing to God any guilt I feel for saying "no" or "not right now"

7. Being still and listening to God (sometimes one of the hardest things to do, but produces the most outcome)

8. Increasing my prayer life, fasting, and time in the Word

9. Being intentional with my time

So I want to challenge you. Are there things you are carrying right now that you need to lay down? Are there commitments you are trying to juggle right now that you simply need to just say no to in this season? Are there ways you need to be more intentional or careful with your time so you can birth the promise of God?

Are there ways you need to narrow your focus?

Write Your Promise Out Clearly

Then the Lord answered me and said, "Write the vision and engrave it plainly on [clay] tablets so that the one who reads it will run" (Habakkuk 2:2 AMP).

"If you can see it, you can have it." When I heard Patricia King say this in one of her sermons, I remember everything in me screaming on the inside, "Yes and amen!" Boy, did I personally walk through that message and learn that it is so true.

Sam and I had just gotten back to the States after being out in the mission field as missionaries with Iris Ministries for over a year. We went from the streets of Calcutta, India and then the rice paddy fields of Nepal to back to living in America.

I remember the first months back being somewhat of a blur of culture shock. We walked into a Starbucks coffee shop one day. After living in the poorest of conditions overseas, being in Starbucks getting a foamy latte of my choice seemed dreamy. A lady in front of me started yelling at the barista for getting her order wrong. In shock and disbelief, I asked her, "Are you okay?" That went over real well! Not! Yep, I was in major culturew shock.

We were back in the states living in Kansas City, Missouri, and we quickly we realized that we needed a vehicle to get around. (Public transportation out here just isn't what it is in other states or nations.) So we started to pray. "Lord, please give us a car. Please do a miracle and provide a vehicle."

Suddenly a few people reached out to us. I distinctly remember a conversation with a beautiful friend. "We have a car that we'd really love to give you. I know you need one. It's kind of a janky car and sometimes has problems and breaks down, but I mean it's something, right?"

God, I thought, *Is this Your answer to our prayers?*

Another person reached out to us. They had a vehicle but the back windows were missing.

Don't read this wrong. I was grateful at that point for anything that could get me from point A to point B. Somewhere inside of me, though, I could sense a small voice saying "I've got better for you. Don't settle."

I'VE GOT BETTER FOR YOU. DON'T SETTLE.

I pressed and prayed. "God what do You have to say about these cars? I need to hear Your voice," I prayed.

His voice responded: "Ana, what is it you actually want? Write it out, believe, and watch what I can do. You don't have to settle."

I could sense the Lord was definitely trying to teach me something here. *Not have to settle,* I pondered. *What would that look like?*

Having been a missionary for years, sometimes barely surviving with just enough food, a wrongful mindset had taught me to just settle. It's funny now, looking back on it. I had been working overseas primarily with orphans, and I myself had an orphan spirit mindset. An orphan mindset thinks in survival mode—"I can only get this scrap or crumb from

God"—instead of just sitting up at His banquet table and partaking in the feast.

"Lord, I'd like a car that I can sit high up in, because I'm short. I want to be able to see better in front of me. I'd like a vehicle that is from the 2000s, not the 1990s. I'd like an automatic car, because, well...You know how my stick-shift driving is. I'd like a car that has AC and heat in it, because the weather out here can be extreme."

Then I added one more thing.

"I'd like that car the little old lady who barely drives has. Low mileage, and a well-kept vehicle. Thank You and amen."

Then I heard, "Write it plainly."

"WRITE IT PLAINLY."

So I did just that. I wrote down all my conditions for the car and began to daily lay hands and decree, declare, and pray over that piece of paper.

Within a week (I kid you not), we were gifted that exact car, which is still our car today!

In Genesis 30 we find an interesting story. Jacob, who had been serving his father-in-law Laban for years, was ready to claim his wages. He said, "Let me pass through your entire flock today, removing from there every speckled or spotted sheep and every black sheep among the lambs, and the spotted or speckled among the goats; and those shall be my wages" (Gen. 30:32).

Jacob then did something interesting! He set down peeled rods that looked stripped in all the areas the flocks would gather to drink and mate. It says in verse 39, "So the flocks mated by the rods, and the flocks delivered striped, speckled, and spotted offspring." Jacob placed the rods near the strongest of the flock, which produced strong spotted offspring—and he prospered.

Isn't that an interesting piece of scripture!

Jacob put within eyesight of the flocks their destiny to be spotted and striped, and voila—it produced the outcome. Let's stop a moment and put into practice this very thing.

I myself have been praying over a promise of God daily, but I feel challenged by my own words here—to "write it plainly," so that I can see it daily, and pray.

What is it you are praying for and contending for? I want to challenge you, don't just settle. You are a son or daughter of the King of kings! You don't have to settle.

Write it out. If you could have the very thing you've been contending for, what specifically would life look like? Be very specific. If God were going to give you exactly what you asked for, what would you ask? Have you lost your eyesight?

Now write it down and post it somewhere you can daily see it and pray over it. You might even have to print out some pictures or draw it out and tape it up on your wall! You should see my office wall right now!

Remember, Habakkuk 2:2 says, "So that the one who reads it will run" (AMP).

Prayer

Lord, I pray for clarity of our eyesight right now. I pray for our focus to get narrowed in on the assignment You have given us in this season. Help us keep our focus. Help us keep our faith for the promise. I declare Revelation 3:18— that we may have eye salve to anoint our eyes so that we may see. God, clarify the direction You are leading us right now. I pray for clarity even over the next steps that we need to take. We want Your perspective and not our own. God, give us Heaven's perspective over this promise right now. Faith! Faith! I declare an increased measure of faith to be imparted to you right now over your destiny! Amen.

CHAPTER 4

Persevere

Persevere.

I must admit, that's probably one of my least favorite words to hear when I'm pressing in faith for my breakthrough. Perhaps it's just me, but when I hear the word *persevere*, I tend to join it in my mind with the words "Looooong process!"

But maybe it's just me.

Persevere means to persist in anything undertaken; maintain a purpose in spite of difficulty, obstacles, or discouragement; continue steadfastly.

So instead of looking at the word *persevere* and thinking it means to be in process for a lengthy time, I'd like to challenge you and myself with the notion that persevering is something so much more. Persevering is standing in faith despite all else.

> # PERSEVERING IS STANDING IN FAITH DESPITE ALL ELSE.

Abraham is considered the father of faith. Despite his own doubt that God could give him a child in his very old age, Abraham believed.

> *He never stopped believing in God's promise, for he was made strong in his faith to father a child. And because he was mighty in faith and convinced that God had all the power needed to fulfill his promises, Abraham glorified God! So now you can see why Abraham's faith was credited to his account as righteousness before God* (Romans 4:20-22 TPT).

Let's just stop and take a moment and imagine the scene. We find his promise in Genesis 15. God came to Abram (who was later named Abraham) in a vision, saying, "Your reward shall be very great" (Gen. 15:1).

Abram responded, "Lord God, what will You give me, since I am childless, and the heir of my house is Eliezer of Damascus?" (Gen. 15:2). (Eliezer was the steward or head servant of Abram's house, and as Abram didn't have a son or heir at the time, his entire inheritance would go to him.)

I love this conversation we see between the Lord and Abram. This man whom we refer to as the "father of faith" wasn't afraid to challenge God and, let's be real, complain to Him a little. "God, You talk of this great reward, but help me fill in the blank here! Where's the reward?"

So God expanded the vision. At the time, Abram was just thinking in terms of one son, one heir, but God opened his eyes to see a much broader picture: "Now look toward the heavens and count the stars, if you are able to count them." And He said to him, "So shall your descendants be."

And then it says, "Then he believed in the Lord."

Abram's faith multiplied in that moment, much further and greater than the level or measure of faith that he had before. And he believed.

Come on! I am so challenged by that statement in itself.

It takes courage to believe a word of God spoken over your life right now, despite what you see in the natural.

There is a reason why God kept telling Joshua and the Israelites to be "strong and courageous" as they crossed into the Promised Land (see Josh. 1:6). You are going to have to push past disbelief and discouragement to take the land.

> **IT TAKES COURAGE TO BELIEVE A WORD OF GOD SPOKEN OVER YOUR LIFE RIGHT NOW, DESPITE WHAT YOU SEE IN THE NATURAL.**

Could you have that level of faith to not only believe God for the very thing you are contending for in this moment, but to believe with vision seeing far beyond that?

See, I believe we need God's perspective to impact this world. We have only a short time here on Earth, and you and I have a part to play in that timeline of history.

There's an invitation for you right now as God says, "Come up here, and I will show you" (Rev. 4:1).

Let's Dream Again

Take a moment and sit with the Lord. Ask Him to show you the vision for the future. Dare to ask Him for where He is taking you.

Get real quiet and ask Him that.

What do you see?

Is it a picture that is full of hope?

Does it provide you direction for this season?

Does it give you a much broader picture to see beyond your current situation you may feel stuck in?

God has plans to give you hope and a future (see Jer. 29:11).

Running with Risk

"Where are the risk takers?" I heard the Lord's booming voice say one day.

Little did I know what He was about to ask me to do. When God said that, I thought He was talking more in broad terms, like where are the risk takers across the earth. I never thought He was pointing the finger right straight at me!

I responded by thinking back, "Well, I'm a risk taker, God."

A voice I know to be the Father's quickly responded. "You have before, and you think you do now. It's time to be stretched," He said.

Uh oh, I thought. *I'm in trouble.*

Times flashed through my mind of being out in the mission field walking through the drug trafficking slums, humming along worshiping Jesus. I remembered chasing angels throughout Brazil to escape possible horrible situations. I remembered when I first stood up to an altar call in the dirt of Mexico at 14 years old, saying yes to be a full-time minister and give my life for the Gospel of Jesus to be preached. The memory flashed through my mind of riding a tiny ski boat at 17 through the ocean with 10-foot waves crashing around us to head out to witness to a group of indigenous people off the coast of Panama with my missions team. I remember saying, "I will marry you," to my husband as he was down on one knee proposing with the largest angel I had ever seen in my life in the sky behind him. Flashing through my mind, I also remembered riding the back of a covered truck bumping along with my husband and team in the pitch darkness of Mozambique, Africa, to go preach the gospel to a group that had never heard the hope of Jesus. That night we saw more crazy wild miracles than I had ever seen before. Then I remembered bringing my two children forth into this world, with all the might I had left, wondering if I would even live past that moment.

Those are the memories that crossed through my mind right then. So "being stretched" seemed a little scary to hear at that moment, if I am being honest. *What on earth does God have in mind now?* I wondered.

We all have our moments of stepping out in faith with God, when our very comfortable walk with Him is challenged. Perhaps you find yourself there right now. Are you being challenged?

This was my moment. I was then taken into a vision that would change the course for my family.

Our Promise

The Lord took me into a vision one day, and showed me a particular land. We walked through a big, open field hand in hand.

"This is your inheritance, Ana," I heard Him say. "You are going to build a place of respite for My front-line workers. It will be a place of peace, a Shiloh. It will be a place of feasting in My Presence and not just settling to get by on My scraps. Ministers will come here and receive clarity of vision from Me for the long haul. This will be a place of encounter. I will bless you with favor as you build, if you obey My words of direction. I want you to build My banquet table, My Casa de la Mesa. In the presence of your enemies, I have set a table for you," He said.

Little did I know how much I was about to be stretched. Going after real estate was definitely a new feat for me. From years of being a missionary, I'd become pretty used to living off whatever God had given me. And He has always been faithful to provide for our family.

And here I was being stretched to see the greater vision. "Ask Me for the land so that you can bless many, many others." God was and is transforming my mind to see beyond myself, to see with His eyes into what will impact not only a region but make an impact on future generations.

Owning real estate of that size and asking for help to purchase it—I found that challenging me to the core.

"It's okay to ask Me for big dreams, Ana," I heard the Lord say to me one morning as I was processing this vision. I had thought I always had, and yet I was being challenged by God to dream way bigger and way beyond anything that I had ever done before.

Before I go on sharing our story, let me just stop and ask you a nudging question from the Holy Spirit.

Do you believe it's okay to dream with God? Do you believe it's okay to ask God for big things?

Do you have a dream?

Some of us have been discouraged for so long that we've put our dreams on an old dusty shelf for safe-keeping, thinking, *Well, when my life looks different, maybe then I can revisit this.*

Then some of us struggle with our own identity as sons and daughters of the King. I found myself in this category being stretched in a much deeper way. Yes, I cast out demons with Jesus; yes, I pray for people and they get delivered and healed; yes, I believe in crazy wild miracles. But somewhere down deep inside, I'd rather dream for myself in a more practical way than actually dream for something this large.

God stretches us beyond where we think we need to grow. Stretching is hard in the process, but as we lean into staying intimate with Him through it, the stretching produces such deep fruit.

IF YOU CAN FIND THAT, THEN YOU PROBABLY HAVE JUST LANDED ON YOUR GOD-GIVEN DESTINY.

So we take leaps and risks with God. Can I challenge you just a little bit more here? What would you do if you could do anything? If there were no limits financially, nothing holding you back physically—what would you do? If you can find that, then you probably have just landed on your God-given destiny.

From the beginning of time, we were called to create with God. Adam and Eve would walk in the Garden of Eden with God and create names of all the new species. This lifestyle of creating with God has been our destiny since we were just dust and an idea in the heart of the Father. Taking risks, though, often involves shedding our pride in every possible way.

Pride

"Ask for the land," I remember He said. "Ask for a huge piece of property."

I pondered, *Why does that make me feel uncomfortable?* Asking is super humbling. Putting my dream with God out there and asking to invite others into it. Fear of rejection was all over it. What will people think of my big dream with God?

Ever been there before?

My pride was being shed just a little more. Risk always means the shedding of pride and leaping in faith with God with no backup plan.

I remember the day like it was yesterday. Sam and I were still newlyweds, in our first year of marriage, without children. We were living in Redding, California, and had heard Heidi and Rolland Baker were coming to speak at our church that weekend.

Long before, the Lord had showed me in a vision that someday my husband and I would go to Mozambique and work as missionaries under Iris Ministries with Heidi and Rolland Baker. So now fast-forward. Heidi and Rolland were visiting our church as speakers that night. They gave an altar call: "Who will lay down their life for the gospel? Who will stop for the one and love the unlovable?" they asked. Just like that, Sam and I knew that word was for us. Grabbing hands, we leaped forward and ran to the front of the altar, not caring who would see us or if it was even an acceptable thing to do. We threw ourselves right down at their feet, and Heidi and Rolland happily laid hands on us and prayed.

The fire of God burned through me that night, and I knew that was a pivotal point in our lives. We had both been missionaries since the age of 17, but this was our first time as a couple. We re-signed up for a life of preaching the gospel. At the time, we didn't care what others thought. There was no ounce of pride in us as we hurtled across rows of chairs to get up at that altar. We wanted God and that was it.

Joseph in the Bible is often an overlooked character as being very pivotal in history, but I look at his story and I see immense courage. He had every opportunity to divorce Mary quietly. To the onlooker, she got pregnant outside of marriage. He had a reason to divorce her. Instead, after having an encounter with a messenger angel and hearing that she was indeed carrying the Son of God, he set aside his pride and took Mary as his wife.

Courage.

It takes immense courage to follow the voice of God. He has ordained your steps and your path. His Word says:

> *When Yahweh delights in how you live your life, he establishes your every step* (Psalm 37:23 TPT).

Asking for Help

I've heard the saying before, "It takes a village to raise a child." The idea of doing things in a group or community is pretty foreign to a western mentality. I still remember when Sam and I were in Africa, and we witnessed a type of community raising that I just hadn't been exposed to in America. I watched as the cutest little African babies would be crying in a service. One of the Mozambican mommas would bring the baby to the momma and the momma would breastfeed it. Then, if she needed help, another momma would step up to help in whatever way was needed—changing the baby, burping the baby, and occasionally, yes, also breastfeeding the baby herself. To me at the time, this was a little bit of a culture clash, yet I still remember it so fondly. It was a beautiful reminder of "it takes a village," and the mommas' sense of community was so deeply rich in their culture.

I believe most of us stay stuck in the place of praying to God for our miracle to descend upon us or praying for change to come. I remember the day that the Lord showed me in a vision a picture of bridges being built around me.

"You're looking for the answer to your dream, but the answers are within reach. They are within grasp, Ana. Look at who I've placed as bridge builders in your life, toward your destiny," I heard Him say.

The paralyzed man in the Bible is a perfect example of this. Jesus was teaching a large group of people and was surrounded. Friends of a man who was paralyzed could not physically get close enough to Jesus with the friend on a stretcher. Desperate to help their friend, they decided to get up on a roof with him and literally lower the man down to land right in front of Jesus (see Luke 5:17-26). In compassion, Jesus commanded the man to pick up his stretcher and walk, and the man was instantly healed.

After Jesus spoke to me that day about bridges, I opened my Bible up and read the story above. I began to realize I was like that man. I was feeling like I literally couldn't get the means I needed for my miracle outside of a move of God, and God was trying to catch my attention.

I am moving! Open your eyes!

The friends of the paralyzed man were like the people the Lord had placed in my life to be the bridges in my path. Some carried knowledge I didn't have, others resources, others just carried me in prayer. As I began to pursue the bridges the Lord had already placed, other bridges were built, other doors opened that previously never could have been. God was in the movement; I just had to realize I wasn't meant to do this alone.

Part of the issue for me was that I wasn't casting the vision to help bring other people along. You aren't meant to do this alone!

YOU AREN'T MEANT TO DO THIS ALONE!

Let's stop and take a moment to reflect with the Holy Spirit. What has the Lord recently spoken to you regarding your promise? What steps has the Lord recently asked you to take? Often we find ourselves stuck because we didn't go back and do the last step He asked us to do.

Who has God placed in your life, even if it's just a recent contact, who may be a bridge builder, who may bring a piece to the puzzle that you hadn't thought of?

Keys to Persevere

Let me take a moment and remind you of the definition of persevere: "to persist in anything undertaken; maintain a purpose in spite of difficulty, obstacles, or discouragement; continue steadfastly."

You know what sticks out to me today about that definition? "In spite of." Perhaps you are like me today. You've been pressing and pressing toward a goal, toward a promise God has shown you, but weariness has set in.

There is a scripture that I have found to be so true. I know, sounds like an oxymoron as all scripture is truth! This one, however, I have witnessed firsthand in my own life to be very true.

> *Hope deferred makes the heart sick, but a longing fulfilled is a tree of life* (Proverbs 13:12 NIV).

Let me give it to you in *The Passion Translation,* because it just breaths new light upon it.

> *When hope's dream seems to drag on and on, the delay can be depressing. But when at last your dream comes true, life's sweetness will satisfy your soul* (Proverbs 13:12 TPT).

So, has weariness set in as you are in the waiting process?

Currently, we've had a day of some breakthrough, but then it seems like at the same time we are back at square one. At a point that felt like a setback, I could feel it creeping back on me. There was weariness like an old friend, all too eager to jump back on me. Something I have been pondering with the Lord now for quite some time is—could hope deferred and weariness be not just an emotion but actually a demonic principality waiting to attach itself? I'm no theologian in this area, but time and time again as I've prayed for people, myself included, and commanded hope deferred and weariness to go in Jesus' name, it physically lifts off people. The person receiving prayer physically looks like the weight of the world has been lifted off their shoulders.

> *Your hand-to-hand combat is not with human beings, but with the highest principalities and authorities operating in rebellion under the heavenly realms. For they are a powerful class of*

*demon-gods and evil spirits that hold this dark
world in bondage* (Ephesians 6:12 TPT).

Perhaps as you are reading this, you may be like I
was today—realizing that it's time to command that
hope deferred and weariness to go in Jesus' name!

Come on, try it out.

The blood of the Lamb was shed for you, so as a
believer in Him, if you have accepted Him into your
heart, that means you have the living Christ inside of
you, and Christ defeated satan and every little principality that he carries.

So it's time that you apply that blood of Jesus and
command: "Weariness and hope deferred, it's time to
go in Jesus' name!"

There now, doesn't that feel better!

What a journey this has been writing a book on
"taking the land," as I am physically walking out the
very core messages and content! Hey, if it works for
me, it's got to help somebody!

Now that we've taken authority over hope deferred
and weariness, I want to share with you a few tips I have
learned through this journey of pressing for a promise
of God for not just my life, but for my family's life.

To be completely transparent with you, there are
plenty of self-help-type books out there on how to persevere. This tip, however, I was surprised by. The Holy

Spirit shared with me that this key is often overlooked but is one of the most powerful and effective keys at unlocking that which has been blocked.

Think of this as a powerful key that will help you unlock destiny! Ready? Drum roll!

Fast!

Yeah! You heard me. Fast! Fasting really does work! Why don't we preach it more in church? Honest moment! I used to be a horrible faster. I've grown up in the church and known that fasting is a good idea to do, but if I was honest it wasn't really a normal part of my lifestyle. I'd go on a 21-day Daniel fast, or once I did a 40-day fast, but it wasn't ever a consistent thing. There have also been times in the past I'd fast for very wrong reasons—feeling pressured because everyone else was, or fasting only for breakthrough to meet my prayer needs. Just being honest.

One day, I came across scripture that changed my perspective on fasting.

In Matthew 6:16-18, Jesus is talking with His disciples and He says:

> *When you fast, don't look gloomy and pretend to be spiritual. They want everyone to know they're fasting, so they appear in public looking miserable and disheveled. Believe me, they've already received their reward. When you fast, don't let*

it be obvious, but instead, wash your face and groom yourself and realize that your Father in the secret place is the one who is watching all that you do in secret and will continue to reward you (TPT).

It wasn't that I hadn't read this scripture before, but it's like the Holy Spirit opened my eyes to see it in a whole different way. I had heard many messages about not broadcasting it to the world when we are choosing to fast and not holding ourselves above others like we own Holy Spirit brownie points. However, the Lord highlighted to me three new thoughts about fasting.

1. "When You Fast" Not "If You Fast"

Jesus said "when" not "if," so it's an indication that fasting was a regular part of the disciples' lifestyle and to be expected. I'm not into pressuring people into doing something just for the sake of being "religious." To me, however, this idea that fasting is to be a regular part of our lifestyles is a game changer. Jesus left instructions for the disciples—those He let into His inner circle—and He left them with the instruction to regularly fast. It isn't about being religious. There are so many rewards we reap when we fast, and Jesus knew it! That's why He said "when," not "if." Game changer! I know!

Maybe you're reading this and are not too convinced yet. Wait until I share with you what happened to me when I regularly started scheduling in fasting as part of my week!

2. *Your Father Is Watching All You Do In Secret*

There is an element of drawing near to the Father through the act of fasting. I don't know about you, but I feel very weak when I fast from food. Not only do I feel weak, but all my weaknesses come right to the surface.

I remember one day, while fasting, my normal patience levels weren't at their best that morning as I watched my five-year-old son take apart our couch for the hundredth time in his life to build what he believed to be the best "structure" ever. (A future engineer in the making I've got here!) The lack of food and coffee was wearing on me. "Son! Really? Do I have to wake up to this every day?" I asked him with an edge to my tone. Immediately, I wanted to take my words back. The look on his face looked so shut down. Despite it being early in the morning, I didn't admire his structure that he had worked so proudly on, and I could tell he felt deflated. I apologized, of course, and immediately began to ooh and ahh and celebrate his creation.

Inwardly, though, I knew there was the impatient side of me God was trying to work with. As I pressed in to Jesus that afternoon, in my prayer time, we met heart to heart. "Let's talk about the condition of your heart," I felt God nudge me. Together we worked on my heart, on areas where I still needed growth.

LET'S TALK ABOUT THE CONDITION OF YOUR HEART.

Through the gift of fasting, I find myself drawing closer to Jesus in my weakness, and He meets me there. God takes the tenderizing process of fasting to draw me closer to Him. Each time I fast, I learn new levels of being more dependent on Him. You will face more and more of your own weaknesses. It's a stripping down, really. Any pride you may have thought you didn't have—but, let's be real, you actually do—you come face to face with through fasting. And that process of being stripped of pride, stripped of normal comforts, and shown our places that still need growth is a great thing!

Fasting is a way of coming clean and repenting before the Lord.

> *They gathered to Mizpah, and drew water and poured it out before the Lord, and fasted on that day and said there, "We have sinned against the Lord." And Samuel judged the sons of Israel at Mizpah* (1 Samuel 7:6).

Realizing our own weakness and lack of perfection before the cross makes us need Him and His forgiveness for our sins all the more.

Looking back over my life, some of my most tender, close encounters with God have come out of seasons when I felt very weak and had to run to Him for strength. And there, in that place, He meets us.

He's meeting you today.

3. He Rewards Those Who Fast!

Not only will you hear God more clearly through fasting, and become more sensitive to His presence, the rewards are legit! Please hear me, though. I have seen people go into fasting (in the past, me being one of them!) for the wrong motives. Instead of fasting to draw near to Him, fasting becomes centered on the idea of "getting my breakthrough." While I do believe breakthrough often comes through fasting, this shouldn't be the end goal. My goal is to draw closer to Him.

> *My beloved is to me the most fragrant apple tree—he stands above the sons of men. Sitting under his grace-shadow, I blossom in his shade, enjoying the sweet taste of his pleasant, delicious fruit, resting with delight where his glory never fades. Suddenly, he transported me into his house of wine—he looked upon me with his*

75

unrelenting love divine (Song of Songs 2:3-4 TPT).

Fasting has nothing to do with getting our way. No, no! It's His Kingdom anyway.

Yet I was surprised at the rewards that did unmistakably come on the days I chose to fast. As you know by now, God gave us this crazy vision to buy land and build a place of peace and respite for prophets and apostles. Buying real estate, especially raw land, in a very aggressive market is no easy feat! But God! As I regularly implemented fasting into my weekly schedule (and as a busy mom, I found that intermittent fasting worked best to keep up with the littles), I recognized that on the days I fasted, more donations seemed to come in for the respite center—the very thing we have been standing in faith for over six years now. God is able!

CHAPTER 5

Stewarding a Prophetic Word

Okay. So God has given you a promise. Now what? What do you do while in that process of waiting for that prophetic word to come to fruition?

What I am about to unpack for you in this single section of the book comes from years of standing on a word of God for our family and our process of carrying that word. All too often we can receive a prophetic word and then do nothing with it, and the word lies dormant. This chapter is meant to encourage you right now, right where you are with some practical, helpful tips.

When you receive a word from God, it's not just your job to wait for it to come to be. It's your job to steward that word, or manage that word. Manage means to bring about or succeed in accomplishing, sometimes despite difficulty or hardship, according to Webster's Dictionary.

God Gives You a Promise

Let's just take a step back, and as a reminder let me unpack the clear word the Lord gave our family. Please don't glance over this, but really read it because I want to show you how and what we did with that word via the Holy Spirit's instruction.

Six years ago now, the Lord showed me a vision first. It's not uncommon for the Lord to speak to me through visions first as I am a seer. (Please see my first book, *The Seer's Path,* if you would like further teaching on how to operate in the gift of a seer.)

I saw a land, and Jesus and I walked in a big open field together hand in hand. "What are You showing me, Lord?" I asked.

"This is your promised land," the Lord said. "This is the land I am giving you to take care of My prophets, apostles, and frontline ministers. It will be a place of peace, a place of respite. It will be a blessing for your inheritance."

Together we walked through that field, and I asked the Lord to show me more of what was on the property.

KEY: ASK THE LORD TO SHOW YOU MORE FOR CLARITY.

The Lord then took me and showed me how the piece of property had aerial views, so mountains were there. I saw large trees off in the distance. The field we walked through was nice and flat to build on with many acres. Then the Lord spoke a scripture to me:

> *You prepare a table before me in the presence of my enemies. You anoint my head with oil; my cup overflows. Surely your goodness and love will follow me all the days of my life, and I will dwell in the house of the Lord forever* (Psalm 23:5-6 NIV).

Again, I asked Him to clarify. Jesus motioned and asked me to come sit down beside Him by a tree, overlooking the field below.

"Ana, I'm asking you to build My banquet table, a place where people will come and just feast in My Presence. They will get filled up, get clarity of vision from Me, and get restored by just feasting in My Presence. And then they will be sent back out into the harvest. With the times that are coming, there will be a need for these places of respite because you and My frontline workers will be pouring out much. You will need a place to tuck back into My Presence. Even I had to tuck away to be with the Father as I poured out."

1. Write It Down

Immediately after I came out of the vision with the Lord, I knew what to do. I picked up my journal and pen and wrote down everything I could remember in detail. And when I say detail, I mean detail. Even down to the smell of the air, to where I saw the sun set, to what the trees looked like if I could draw them out. I wrote down everything, even how I felt after the Lord had asked me to build this place. I wrote down the scripture and actually copied it in big bold letters in my journal, and on my desk, and on my wall so I could have a daily reminder.

Habakkuk 2:2-3 says:

> *Then the Lord replied: "Write down the revelation and make it plain on tablets so that a herald may run with it. For the revelation awaits an appointed time; it speaks of the end and will not prove false. Though it linger, wait for it; it will certainly come and will not delay"* (NIV).

Do you know why it is so important, when God speaks something to us, to write it down in detail? Later, when the enemy's voice seems so much louder or when others may come with confusing or conflict-ing opinions or you may even doubt yourself in the struggle to stand in faith, you will have that word to stand on! Especially if you have been contending for a long time for something, as I know you have. You will need that word to reflect back on for clarity and say, "What exactly was it that God said to me anyway?"

Did you hear that?

Take a moment right now, stop, and get clarity. Ask yourself: "What was it that God originally said to me?"

During this process of seeking the Lord for the promised land, it was so easy at times to wonder, "God, could this be it? Is this the promise? Well, maybe…"

God is specific if we ask Him. Sometimes the biggest battleground is in the place of our mind. We doubt and wonder—did we really hear Him correctly? We can even misconstrue something to hopefully fit the word God gave us in our passion and discontent during the process of preparing that blessing.

Did you just say amen! (Yeah, I heard you!)

That's why you need to write down what you hear in detail. Like a treasure map, one day you will be able to glance back over all the small ways the Lord has been speaking to you over the years about this promise in detail. This will be your greatest key or confirmation and provide for you the reassurance to step forward.

2. Pray for Clarity and Direction

The Lord makes firm the steps of the one who delights in him; though he may stumble, he will

not fall, for the Lord upholds him with his hand.
I was young and now I am old, yet I have never
seen the righteous forsaken (Psalm 37:23-25
NIV).

The Lord will not cause you to fall! Cast your fear of falling on Him right now. Cast all your fears of failing as you jump out in faith at the foot of His cross. He will carry you! Do you believe that? God will not abandon you to figure this out on your own. He is carrying you through to the promise.

Now is the time to get clarity. You have been praying and contending for a while now, and now is the time to ask for clarity. Often we can be moving so quickly, staying so focused on one thing, one goal, that we lack the ability to stand back and see the whole picture from a distance.

Pride.

There, I said the word.

Can we just stop and be honest here for a moment? Sometimes our own pride gets in the way of us seeking clarity and direction, as we are afraid to admit that we could have made a mistake.

When pride comes, then comes disgrace, but with
humility comes wisdom (Proverbs 11:2 NIV).

"God, I thought I heard You and knew which way I was going, but maybe I was actually wrong? God, maybe I heard You and applied that word to what I wanted to be right, what I wanted to fit, but it isn't actually Your best for me."

Ouch. Be willing to ask the Lord for clarity of the promise right now, and also the steps He is asking you to take in walking toward it.

Admittedly, many times in carrying this word for the past six years, I have had to go back to God and ask for clarity as I sometimes wrongly thought, *This must be the land. Does this fit the vision?* It's been such a process of really having to press in to Him to get clarity and walk humbly, admitting several times to my interces- sors, "Perhaps I am wrong on this property."

And yet the promise is still there. And yet you do hear the voice of God. And yet He still loves you!

Take a moment to pause and pray for God to bring clarity and direction today.

3. Submit to Authority and Spiritual Mentors

Right from the very beginning of receiving this vision from the Lord, we heard Holy Spirit encourage us to submit it to the people who have authority in our lives.

What has been amazing is to have people who have real wisdom, and who have gone before us and pioneered and walked through many moves of God, speak into our very lives. These are people who truly care for our family and will prophetically go before the Lord and hear direction for us. Without fear they will share what they hear from the Lord with us, even if it doesn't line up with what we are hearing. Pulling counsel into the process of walking out your promise is so necessary!

Hold on tightly to the people in your life who are willing to love you, challenge you, and call you up higher to a deeper place with God.

4. Apply the Word

For the word of God is alive and active. Sharper than any double-edged sword, it penetrates even to dividing soul and spirit, joints and marrow; it judges the thoughts and attitudes of the heart (Hebrews 4:12 NIV).

Jesus answered, "It is written: 'Man shall not live on bread alone, but on every word that comes from the mouth of God'" (Matthew 4:4 NIV).

You will also declare a thing, and it will be established for you; so light will shine on your ways (Job 22:28 NKJV).

For the Lord gives wisdom; from his mouth come knowledge and understanding (Proverbs 2:6 NIV).

So also will be the word that I speak; it does not return to me unfulfilled. My word performs my purpose and fulfills the mission I sent it out to accomplish (Isaiah 55:11 TPT).

I just wanted to start off this section by listing a couple of scriptures in the Bible that point to the power of using God's Word. The Word of God is such a strong weapon when we are in battle, and yet the church has lost sight of using it. Jesus Himself, when led into the desert, combatted the enemy and defeated him by using the Word of God ("It is written"). If anything, that alone should cause us to be passionate about using the Word more. If it worked for Jesus, it will work for you!

And mind you, in case you forgot—we are in a battle!

> *For our struggle is not against flesh and blood, but against the rulers, against the authorities, against the powers of this dark world and against the spiritual forces of evil in the heavenly realms* (Ephesians 6:12 NIV).

The promise, the very thing you have been contending over for so long now, is all part of God's beautiful plan. This isn't about you getting your wish. Of course God knows the desires of our hearts, and He loves them. At some point in your walk with Him, out of your love relationship with Jesus, you will start to realize it's not really about you anymore. He's King, and this is His Kingdom. As you start to grow more in love with Him, your prayers and desires will begin to change into:

*Your kingdom come, your will be done, on earth
as it is in heaven* (Matthew 6:10 NIV).

The very promise that you are believing for today is
all a part of God's Kingdom manifesting here on earth.
You are a part of His story. The very thing you are walking through, right now, you will help others someday
get victory in. God will use your life, if you are willing,
to do something magnificent for His glory!

YOU ARE A PART OF HIS STORY.

The enemy of this world wants nothing more than
to stop you from fulfilling that promise. The devil's very nature is to steal, kill, and destroy—yes, even
your dreams!

Let's take a moment together and do some combat.
Feeling a little discouraged today? Perhaps you should
do as I'm about to—get out the Word of God, march
around your house (or your yard, as I'm going to do),
and decree and declare out loud over your situation
what God says.

In the next chapter, you will write an amazing declaration using the Word. It's time to get it out, and let's
wave that sword back in the enemy's face.

Watch and see what the power of the Word does!

5. Sow into the Vision

One day, I woke up and heard a clear word from the Lord. I love when God does that. Couldn't every day be like that, where you just wake up and immediately hear His voice? It sure would make life a bit easier!

He said, "Sow into the vision."

Then during my morning devotional time that day, I stumbled across this little verse in the Bible that's like a sucker-punch wake-up call of a verse!

> *Do not be deceived, God is not mocked; for whatever a person sows, this he will also reap* (Galatians 6:7).

The scripture goes on to talk about doing good for other people, but the notion of sowing and reaping stuck out to me as I knew the Lord was trying to get my attention regarding the land.

Sowing and reaping isn't a new concept for me. It's not always just about finances; it could be your time, your energy, or simply serving someone. You will reap the rewards of it later.

Recently, I was doing a television show with Katie Souza along with many other guests. Her staff had their hands full with all the scheduled filming, and unfortunately James Goll was supposed to be coming in that next day and had no one to transport him from the hotel to the studio—about a 45-minute drive away. I eagerly volunteered, as he's my spiritual papa and friend. Boy, did we have such a wonderful time that day in the car talking about prophetic history and just catching up as he asked about my husband and kids and I asked about his new grandbaby!

On the way back as I was talking with James, he stopped, cocked his head to the side as he often does when he's getting a prophetic word of the Lord, and said to me, "You're reaping the blessing now from serving Katie's ministry. Things are opening for you now as you are coming under her atmosphere of faith." And it was true! That day, I gained more understanding of the concept of reaping what you sow and the blessing that comes from servanthood.

Let's fast-forward now. When I woke up that morning and heard clearly from the Lord, "Sow into the vision," and the scripture was highlighted to me of reaping and sowing, I knew that God was asking us to do a little something more than just pray.

Financially, we needed to sow. As we prayed and the Lord led us to, we started to sow our money (outside of our normal tithes) to certain projects and ministries that we believed were ushering in the Presence of the Lord. As we would sow, we would pray, "Lord, let this be a blessing to them, and let it be a blessing toward our land."

Every time we sowed, we reaped. Clearer vision would come, God would send people in our path who would connect with us—all keys toward us getting the land. It really does work; you really will reap what you sow! So consider even today sowing through your finances into the very thing you are contending for.

> *"Bring the whole tithe into the storehouse, so that there may be food in My house, and put Me to the test now in this," says the Lord of armies, "if I do not open for you the windows of heaven and pour out for you a blessing until it overflows"* (Malachi 3:10).

6. Prayer and Fasting! It Really Works!

> *But as for you, when you pray, go into your inner room, close your door, and pray to your Father who is in secret; and your Father who sees what is done in secret will reward you* (Matthew 6:6).

"Just pray," I heard the Lord tell me one day, as I had let my mind wander and ponder the questions: *Why aren't we getting breakthrough yet? Why the delay? Is this ever going to happen, Lord? Do You still have this promise for our family?*

Rest assured, all of us—and I repeat, all of us—struggle with doubt at some point along the process of pressing in for a promise of God. It's the number-one way the enemy hits us and tries to take our faith out!

But He commanded me that day, "Just pray." I got the memo! Stop complaining and worrying, and just go pray! At least that's how I internalized it.

I went in my office, shut the door, sat down in my favorite comfy prayer chair, and met with the Lord in prayer. The minute I did this, guess what happened? The worries, doubts, and fears all lifted off of me. I physically felt lighter, and although I didn't have answers, the assurance that God's got this and He's in control returned!

As I started to also mix weekly fasting into my prayer time with the Lord over the land, we started to see immense change. Mostly the breakthrough I saw was over the mental battle of contending for an extended amount of time. It was so much easier to remain victorious over discouragement and stand in faith as I turned to prayer and fasting. Another tip—write down your prayer requests in a journal. Looking back weekly and seeing how He responded in His own way was so much fun!

7. Remind God

As weird as this sounds (like, why would you need to remind God of anything? He's all-knowing, right?), it's biblical to pray prayers reminding God of His promises. Moses did it, so why can't you?

In Exodus 32, Moses had just received the two tablets written from the Lord Himself for the Israelites up on Mount Sinai, and then he discovered that the Israelites had made other golden idols to worship in their frustration over how long it took Moses to come down the mountain. In God's anger toward the people, He planned to wipe out the Israelites all together and start over.

> *Now leave Me alone, that My anger may burn against them and that I may destroy them; and I will make of you a great nation* (Exodus 32:10).

Moses then intervened on behalf of the Israelites and reminded God of His promise to the people.

> *"Turn away from Your burning anger and change Your mind about harming Your people. Remember Abraham, Isaac, and Israel (Jacob), Your servants to whom You swore [an oath] by Yourself, and said to them, 'I will multiply your descendants as the stars of the heavens, and all this land of which I have spoken I will give to your descendants, and they shall inherit it forever.'" So the Lord changed His mind about the harm which He had said He would do to His people* (Exodus 32:12-14 AMP)

What? Did you read that? God changed His mind because Moses reminded Him of His promise.

So, I dare you. Pray prayers today reminding God of the promised word He has spoken over you.

8. Directly Obey

If God commands you to do something, obey Him directly without compromise. Obeying without compromise brings the favor of the Lord, and the favor of the Lord brings blessing. Do you want the blessing of the Lord over your life? Then do not compromise. Just obey.

(On a side note, I think this should be the next t-shirt slogan that takes off. Those of us who lived through the '80s remember the message of "Just Do It" on t-shirts. Well I say, "Just obey!")

God gave us a vision for this promised land over six years ago. One thing He very specifically instructed us was, "Do not cast the vision for this until I release you to. You aren't to ask people for donations for it until I say it's time."

We received that command, and then the onslaught of temptations to raise donations came directly following that. (It often happens that when you receive a command from the Lord, a temptation to disobey usually follows directly after.)

A friend called me up with a plan. This was a friend the Lord had allowed us to share with and ask for prayer. She had the best intentions and wanted so deeply to help us.

The plan she had come with unfolded into something of a donation drive—a way to campaign and get the word out there about the vision, etc. I so appreciated her heart, but I knew we weren't released to do that.

"Lean not on your own understanding" was the word I kept hearing Holy Spirit whisper after that phone call (see Prov. 3:5).

A year later, I found myself ministering at a meeting in Texas. No one there (outside of Joan Hunter) knew about this land we had been praying for. Another prophet there looked at me from the pulpit and started prophesying, "Ana, I see the builder's anointing over you. You are going to build a place of safety and shalom peace, a bethel for leaders in the Body of Christ. The land is there. You need the finances, but the finances are there. You will build this. The Lord's favor and blessing is over you and your family to build this."

The easy thing to do in that moment would have been to agree with him and perhaps draw attention to the fact that we needed the finances—"Yes Lord, do it, God!"—but I did not. Please hear me out. You see, God hadn't released us yet to even share this vision with many people. I nodded, thanked the prophet, and later told him what a confirmation of the Lord his word was, but I drew no attention to it and I didn't share it with the crowd there.

A year later, one morning while in the shower, I heard the Lord's voice, "Now is the time to cast the vision."

Shocked, I replied, "No, Lord!"

You see, we had done such a great job of stewarding the word, and only sharing it with the few people the Lord allowed us to share with, that sharing our beautiful promise almost felt too vulnerable now.

But we obeyed. Looking back on all of this process, I realize now that the timing of the Lord was perfect. We had so much clarity at the time and felt very grounded. Now the timing is right for our family to move locations, which wouldn't have been the right timing prior to this. The purpose—to build a place of respite for frontline ministers—is now in the right place on the timeline of God. Now more than ever we need ministers to run into the frontlines of battle and declare the hope and glory of Jesus. Those ministers, including me, will need a place to tuck back after pouring out and get replenished so we can run back out into the frontlines again, full of God leaking out of our very beings!

WILL YOU OBEY GOD WHEN OPPORTUNITY COMES KNOCKING?

I believe there is a challenge presented right now to the Body of Christ. Will you obey God when opportunity comes knocking?

My sheep hear my voice, and I know them, and they follow me (John 10:27 NKJV).

9. Rightly Aligned—Get Your Faith On!

As a parent, I am well aware of the fact that who my kids are friends with—and also what they take in through what they see or hear—directly affects who they become. That's why we are so protective of what influences our kiddos!

In the same way, as I mentioned before, it is so important that you are careful whom you allow into the birth room of this promise of God over your life. You cannot trust everyone to hear the voice of God for you! Although they may be loving people and really, truly care for you, this care sometimes can override their ability to hear God clearly, causing them to just ride off of emotions.

Ask God for a few faith-filled friends who will build up your faith, encourage you through the valleys of discouragement or disappointment, and also who aren't afraid to challenge you if they hear differently. Align yourself with people who are filled with faith and can look past the impossibility that may seem to be blaring itself in your face right now. Those are the ones you need praying with you right now. That's who you need to seek counsel from.

I hear you. You might say, "But Ana, I don't have anyone like that in my life right now." Another way you can align yourself with a faith-filled person is to come under their ministry. Study their books, do a school of theirs if one is available, find a way to bless them—whether it be to financially bless them or even just write them a letter of gratitude. As you sow into their ministry, in a way you are aligning yourself with them.

10. Remember Your History with God

Last, but perhaps one of the most important steps (well, actually, each step is super important), is that along this process of walking into your promise of God, which sometimes can feel like you are trudging up a giant mountain, look back in gratefulness and recall all the times that God has been faithful in your life.

This has been one of the most helpful keys I have learned while contending for the past six years. At every point of discouragement, the enemy would like nothing more than for you to look at your situation and not see the progress you have made.

God gave to the Israelites a command after they crossed the Jordan—to pick 12 stones out of the very middle of the Jordan as an act of remembrance. It was to remind the people and their children of how God had miraculously brought them into the Promised Land.

This shall be a sign among you; when your children ask later, saying, "What do these stones mean to you?" then you shall say to them, "That the waters of the Jordan were cut off before the ark of the covenant of the Lord; when it crossed the Jordan, the waters of the Jordan were cut off." So these stones shall become a memorial to the sons of Israel forever (Joshua 4:6-7).

When I came across this scripture, the Lord showed me that although the Israelites did this once they had crossed over the Jordan, it would help me to similarly remember His faithfulness throughout my whole life and thank Him through the process of getting to our promise.

Right now, I have no doubt that you are very close to crossing over. If your promise wasn't close, Holy Spirit wouldn't have a divine plan for your eyes to read over this section about the Israelites crossing over the Jordan into their promised land. But this is the time when discouragement can be the greatest.

Now is the time to take a moment and look back over your lifetime and draw on those memories of how faithful God has been to pull you through all your life.

The second part of this key is to take a moment to stop and thank Him for His faithfulness. Trust me, I know what I'm writing! Each time I have felt discouraged, and I turned away from that discouragement to thank God for moments He had been faithful in my life, discouragement slowly melted away. It gave me the endurance to keep going, to keep climbing that mountain and not agree with hopelessness.

> ## IT GAVE ME THE ENDURANCE TO KEEP GOING, TO KEEP CLIMBING THAT MOUNTAIN AND NOT AGREE WITH HOPELESSNESS.

So do it with me now. Don't stop until you feel released to. You can pick up as many memorial stones as you need today! Remember your history with God.

Thank You, Jesus, for the time You _____

_____

_____

Thank You, Jesus, for bringing this good thing into my life _____

_____

_____

Thank You, Jesus, for _____

_____

_____

Be careful that you do not forget the Lord who brought you out of the land of Egypt, out of the house of slavery (Deuteronomy 6:12).

CHAPTER 6

Overthrow Giants in the Land

Anyone who has ever had to contend for a specific promise God has for them has had to overthrow some giants! Giants are the demonic attacks that often hold us back, can hold us in bondage to fear, or just completely block us from walking in our destiny! I remind you that the enemy wants to do nothing more than stop you from walking forward!

I've noticed a pattern when it comes to my own moments of breakthrough throughout my life, and perhaps you can relate. Right before a huge breakthrough or promotion comes, often a whole heap of warfare comes to try and stop that breakthrough.

Breakthrough doesn't come without warfare! If you aren't experiencing warfare in some measure, I'd encourage you to dream bigger and larger. Stretch those faith muscles!

I remember one day when I was heading out to go film a television show series with Kevin Zadai. On my way out the front door, something literally knocked me down those three icy steps. There I was, wincing in pain at 4 a.m. on the front stoop—because of course all flights seem to leave Kansas City in the wee hours of the morning.

"You've got to do better than that to knock me out, devil!" I said out loud angrily as I pulled myself off the ground. I ended up filming that first day with bruising still on my arms. Talk about warfare!

Warfare can also set in right after a huge promotion or breakthrough. The enemy is cunning, you see. He'll slam you with warfare afterward, and this tempts you to shy away and not advance toward that very area of promise God's calling you to walk in. You may have a huge advancement or what feels like breakthrough toward your promise, and then come home to unrest in the home. Warfare.

The encouraging news is—do you find yourself right now in a bit of warfare? There's hope! Perhaps you are very close to your promise of God. Now is not the time to quit! Keep advancing forward in steps of faith, even if they are steps through weakness.

Your little yes is still a yes and God will reward your obedience to keep taking steps forward that He is showing you.

Moses sent a few spies ahead to go and check out the Promised Land of Canaan, just to see what they were up against. Not a bad idea if you ask me, but more on that later!

> *See what the land is like, and whether the people who live in it are strong or weak, whether they are few or many* (Numbers 13:18).

The spies returned and gave a full report:

> *We came into the land where you sent us, and it certainly does flow with milk and honey, and this is its fruit. Nevertheless, the people who live in the land are strong, and the cities are fortified and very large. And indeed, we saw the descendants of Anak there!* (Numbers 13:27-28)

Giants! There were giants in the land!

Sometimes our promise, the very thing we were meant to face, looks like fortified impossibility. *How will I ever accomplish this, Lord? How can You make a way when this looks impossible?*

"Impossibility" itself will be the very first giant you and I have to face down. Jesus said:

> *With people this is impossible, but with God all things are possible* (Matthew 19:26).

All things! Yep, even that thing that is staring you right in the face today—even that! All things are possible with God.

Big promises require big faith. And faith is often acquired through testing. Perhaps you are being tested right now.

FAITH IS OFTEN ACQUIRED THROUGH TESTING.

Our Testing: Big Promises, Big Faith

As I am writing this book right now, I am facing my very own season of testing. My husband and I went out searching to find the land the Lord showed us in our vision, but once we found that promised land, that was just a tiny bit of the real battle.

The Israelites were commanded to overthrow the giants after crossing over into the Promised Land (see Num. 33:52). I think it's interesting that the Israelites saw the Promised Land before they went in to capture it. Mentally going in to capture it was the real battle.

Back to our land. We found a beautiful piece of property, one that so uniquely stood out by itself. My father, who went with us, phrased it so perfectly: "Wow, it's so peaceful up here!"

Our vision was to establish a place for prophets and apostles to get rest, peace, and vision with the Lord, so this seemed like the perfect land. Its beauty was breathtaking. Its expanse was an enormous canvas. I might add, it also looked like a ton of work! *Could this be it?* we began to wonder excitedly. *Over six years of waiting for this promise to come to pass, and could this really be our promised land?*

And then we faced our biggest mountain that seemed like impossibility—the expense. We have currently raised half the amount required to attain the land. "Not nearly enough," said the current landowner as he laughed at our offer.

"But God, You showed me this promise. You asked me to take steps of faith, and I've done everything I know to do. Lord, would You move this mountain?" I asked in prayer one morning.

Nothing. Not a budge from the landowner.

I'm sharing with you our own journey of standing in faith as a family, throughout this book, to show you that I'm in this too! I'm contending right now. I'm not on the other side of this mountain; I'm not walking in my promise of God yet.

GOD HAS THE FINAL SAY!

But I still believe. And I believe for you too. God has the final say! Even if everything seems closed right now and every door seems shut in your face—God has a plan and a purpose in all of this.

Some teachers share only after their victories. I tend to be a parabolic prophet—meaning I go through and walk out the very message the Lord is prophetically giving me.

I believe today is your day to slay some giants, starting with a few named fear, disappointment, hopelessness, weariness, doubt, and defeat.

While, yes, there may be other things standing in your way—perhaps even finances, like in our case, is a giant for you too—but I believe that the really big giants standing in your way are fear, disappointment, hopelessness, weariness, and doubt. The enemy will use those five to stop you from advancing forward if you give them too much of your attention.

The mountain looks intimidating before you right now. "How, God? I believe You can, I just can't see how," might be the question you are wrestling with.

Evicting Defeat

As I am writing this for you, I hear the Holy Spirit say, "It's time to pull yourself up off the ground." Not in your own strength, of course, but Jesus will help you. You are not defeated.

> *In Jesus' name, I pray and break the power of a spirit of defeat that has been following the one who is reading this. I release the truth over you— that in Christ you are victorious. I speak 2 Corinthians 4:8-9 over you: You are hard pressed*

in every way possible, but not crushed. You may feel struck down, but you are not destroyed. You are not abandoned in this process of contending for your promise from God. You are not defeated. Amen.

IT'S TIME TO PULL YOURSELF OFF THE GROUND. JESUS WILL HELP YOU.

Sometimes you are going to need to use the Word of God, worship, and thanksgiving to get yourself off the floor of defeat. Here is my own personal account of facing down defeat and eventually evicting him. (Yep, I said "him" because defeat is a spirit!)

I had hit a low moment in my journey of standing in faith. I promise there were high moments too! We all go through both the valleys and the pinnacles in our journey with faith. But I hope that sharing the vulnerable stuff and what helped me get out of the low place will also help you if you are in that place today.

I was feeling totally defeated. We thought we had found the land, but it turned out it wasn't. (More on that later.) So, feeling defeated and my faith deflated, I had to find a scripture to stand on and help dig me out of the trenches of discouragement.

"I can do all things through Christ who strengthens me" (Phil. 4:13 NKJV) became the scripture that

I used like a sword to help me get out of the dumps of defeat.

I encourage you, reader, to go get your Bible out and find a scripture to march around and declare over yourself when you feel defeat drawing near.

Another key to evicting defeat is worship. Pushing myself in front of my keyboard and forcing myself to worship Jesus, even when I didn't feel like it, really did help.

David did it when he was in total dismay running from Saul. There he was, the future king, hiding in caves. Talk about being in a valley! Singing psalms of praise to God helped him war against defeat, so why shouldn't it help you too!

The song "Remember" by Bryan and Katie Torwalt is the worship song that most helped me face down defeat. I encourage you to crank up the volume and go listen to it.

"Remember"
by Bryan and Katie Torwalt

How quickly we forget the God
who lives in every day
How easy to lose sight that You
reside in the mundane
How quickly we forget the power
that's running through our veins

The kind of power that empties graves

And oh my soul

Remember who you're talking to

The only one who death bows to

That's the God who walks with you

And oh my soul

You know that if He did it then

He can do it all again

His power can still raise the dead

Don't tell me that He's finished yet.

How to Slay a Giant

I'd like to point out some practical tips that I am doing daily to slay my giants of fear, disappointment, weariness, and doubt that creep up right now, as I have yet to take possession of our promised land.

1. *The Word*

> *It is written: "Man shall not live on bread alone, but on every word that comes out of the mouth of God"* (Matthew 4:4).

> *For the word of God is living and active, and sharper than any two-edged sword* (Hebrews 4:12).

By now, I'm guessing that you know the importance of reading the Word of God daily, and you may even also know the importance of decreeing and declaring the Word of God out loud over yourself. But can I ask you something? Do you really actually do it?

One morning during my prayer time with the Lord, I felt challenged by Him. He said, "Ana, I want you to write out a written declaration using scripture about the land, and I want you to say it daily out loud. You're not declaring daily over the promise—My word."

Oh—ouch! It was true. I'd spent much time praying about it and conversing with the Lord and also close friends about the land. I knew that using the Word of God would speak life into the situation when all looked bleak, but I wasn't actually doing it.

That's when I sat down and dug into the Word of God and handwrote out our own declaration. Here's what I wrote, just as an example. I really do encourage you to dig into the scriptures and write out your own.

> *I declare that God will meet all our needs according to His riches in glory by Christ Jesus. All finances that are needed to take ownership of the land, God will fulfill. We will take ownership of it, and the land will be granted peace. I declare that it will be a place of encounter with the presence of the Lord, and be a place of rest. It will be a banquet table, a place where people can come and feast at the Lord's table and get filled up. The land will be guaranteed to bless my descendants.*

By faith, I claim that it is ours and has the Lord's seal of approval over it. Hallelujah!

When I started using the Word of God as a sword and started daily reading my declaration out loud, as I read it I could feel those giants of hopelessness and discouragement leave the room. It's amazing how it actually works! Using the Word of God and declaring it out loud literally causes the devil to flee! Each time I decree it out loud, I feel like little David flinging my little sling with pebble stones over my head and aiming them right at the enemy's forehead. I can feel my faith rise up each time I decree it.

Let's stop a moment before I give you the next key. Take a moment and write out your own declaration using the Word. Make sure it's personal—write it in your own words and the way you talk with God. Post it up somewhere you will see it every day.

2. *Worship*

Psalm 100:4 says we "enter His gates with thanksgiving, and His courtyards with praise. Give thanks to Him, bless His name."

When all looks hopeless, bless Him. When you feel so discouraged and feel like just quitting, thank Him. When you doubt if you even heard God correctly because it has been so long with no victory in sight, worship Him!

Trust me, it shifts something. I remember one day when my spiritual eyes were opened to see exactly what happens when we worship. I had gone through a solid six weeks of not being able to hear the voice of God. (As a prophet, that's a little scary!) All I could hear was the voice of the accuser speaking loudly. All day, every day for six weeks straight, I could feel a demonic presence following me around, and the lies would start up.

"You are losing the best years of your life with your children."

"You're not being a good enough momma to your daughter."

Lies! Six weeks! Six weeks it continued on!

In the middle of the night one night, I woke up and felt the demonic presence again right near me in my room. In my desperation, I went downstairs and cried out to God.

"God! I can't hear You. I know there's something following me around, trying to accuse me, trying to get me to quit at ministry. I know they are lies, but I need to hear the truth from You, God! Where are You, God?"

Just then, I began to worship. Can I be real with you? It wasn't the prettiest, most profound song. No, no! What came out was a simple song, through sobs— but it was pure worship. Straight from my heart, not dressed up with flashy lights or smoke machines. Pure worship.

Suddenly in that moment, my spiritual eyes were opened, and I could see the swirl of demons that had been assigned to me. I could see them all throughout the room. As I worshiped, suddenly they shrieked and ran away!

Did you catch that? They shriek and shrink back at the sound of your worship.

But let's be real here. Sometimes we have to choose worship. It doesn't come easily; you may not feel like doing it because, well, life is just really hard right now— yet you just choose to do it. Don't wait until you feel like worshiping. Just do it. Every time we stop and praise Him and thank Jesus for His goodness despite our feelings, we do war against the enemy of this world.

So in this season, as I am waiting for my promise of God, worship is my weapon. When I feel the discouragement come on, I go into my office, shut the door behind me, turn on my keyboard, and begin to sing. Currently, I am learning to take the scriptures, read them, and sing them out. I'm grateful for people like Julie Meyer, who has personally inspired me to sing the scriptures. (Her latest book, *30 Days of Praying the Psalms: King David's Keys for Victory*, is excellent!)

As I worship through discouragement, I feel Him draw near. As He draws near, I felt peace come over me despite not having answers. His good and perfect peace meets me in my place of weakness.

As I "thank You, Jesus" for the good things that are in my life, my eyes are cast above the current storm. My perspective is shifted from my lack in this season to my past victories with God. I am reminded of His faithfulness. As I wrote in my journal:

> I have found you in the place where I am broken.
>
> I have found you in the place where I'm in need.
>
> I have found you in the place of my surrender.
>
> And I have found you best on my knees.

3. *Prayer*

> *Ask, and it will be given to you; seek, and you will find; knock, and it will be opened to you* (Matthew 7:7).

Did you know? There is a literal room in Heaven where our answers to prayers are sitting on shelves like parcels, lining the walls as far as your eyes can see, and angels are just waiting for their instruction from King Jesus to release those answers on earth.

Jesus took me there one day. I saw some angels standing on the sidelines just waiting. Questioning this in my heart, Jesus heard my thoughts and answered, "They are waiting for My saints down below to pray and ask for what it is they need. For you see, these are the answers to their prayers, yet some are afraid to ask."

Prayer really, actually works! The timing of Heaven is different from the way we look at it as humans. God sees yesterday, today, and tomorrow. So the way time is viewed in Heaven is so different from how we see it on earth. Think of it this way. You and I, once we pass away, just go on to live in eternity. I was trying to explain it to my eight-year-old daughter just the other day. She's grappling with the fact that people die and that we don't last forever.

"Well," I said. "Yes, our bodies don't last, but then we just go on to live in Heaven, so really we live forever. It's what we do with our time here on Earth that matters now."

So when you go in secret and pray, know this— you're prayers are heard and God is releasing an answer. That answer might look different from the outcome you are seeking, because we can't see from His perspective and timeline. He is still good, and He is still in control.

Can I challenge you? What if your answer is waiting there in Heaven for you to pray the prayer to release it?

What is it really you are contending for right now? Those are the prayers that need to be released. Full-of-faith prayers!

See, I believe God is waiting for us to step into our inheritance and start praying the prayers that really demand faith. Also, when you dream with God, and dream beyond just for yourself, anything is possible with Him.

IT'S TIME FOR YOU TO GET A GOD DREAM!

It's time for you to get a God dream!

4. Stand on the Promise

Therefore, take up the full armor of God, so that you will be able to resist on the evil day, and having done everything, to stand firm (Ephesians 6:13).

One of my favorite scriptures in the Bible is where Moses faces his fear from the very beginning. God asks Moses to throw his staff down, and as he does it, it becomes a snake.

Later, that very staff would become the item God used to have Moses plunge into the ocean and split the Red Sea with.

As I've meditated on the life of Moses over and over, it gives me hope. He's a character in the Bible who is full of faith right from the start. Nope! That's a typo right there! When God asked Moses to con-front Pharaoh and help deliver the Israelites from the Egyptians, Moses' first response is, "Who, me? But I have this stuttering problem God! I can't speak before people!" (I paraphrased here but it's pretty close!)

> ## MOSES' VERY PLACE THAT WAS TESTED BEFORE IS WHAT HE USED TO PASS THROUGH IN VICTORY LATER.

My friend, faith builds upon itself. I believe faith is like currency. As you pass through one trial, you can cash in that moment when you chose to stand in faith for the greater test that's coming. Moses' very place that was tested before is what he used to pass through in victory later. Remember the staff!

God will test you in the small first, to see what you do with it. Where's your faith? Then later, when you have passed that test, you can look back and say, "Remember, God, when I passed that trial; if I can trust You in that, then I can trust You in this bigger test. You will come through for me!"

As I've been personally praying for you (I literally prayed for the reader who would get their hands on this book), you know what I kept seeing in a vision? I saw a person standing with their feet firmly planted on the ground. I watched as I saw the ground start shaking with mini-quakes underneath, but their stance was unmoved.

Right now, you are facing many challenges, many moments when you could doubt. There is a war over your stance right now. Will you be moved by doubt? Will you give in to doubt? This season right now of crossing into the promised land is going to take people who have some grit, who have the tenacity and faith to say, "No, this is what God told me and I will not settle for less!"

Often the enemy will use people to speak doubt into the situation. Open your ears to wisdom, but close your ears to doubt. You may have to pray, "Is this wisdom speaking right now, or is this doubt trying to sway me off my target?"

THIS IS WHAT GOD TOLD ME AND I WILL NOT SETTLE FOR LESS!

Here are some faith scriptures I've meditated on when I needed to build myself up and feel encouraged:

> *In hope against hope he believed* (Romans 4:18).
>
> *My sheep hear My voice, and I know them, and they follow Me* (John 10:27).
>
> *Do not worry about your life* (Luke 12:22).

Now faith is the assurance of things hoped for, the conviction of things not seen (Hebrews 11:1 ESV).

Perfect love casts out fear (1 John 4:18 NKJV).

So do me a favor, literally as a prophetic act—stand up if you can, and say out loud (as there is power in your words), "I choose faith, and I will not waver!"

A pattern I have repeatedly seen firsthand is that right before a breakthrough or promotion in the spirit comes intensified warfare. That's why it is so important, as you are pressing for a breakthrough, that you ask a few people to cover you in prayer. It has been my experience that more prayer coverage equals less warfare.

MORE PRAYER COVERAGE = LESS WARFARE

Even now as I write this, I can feel the warfare around our family intensifying. Discouragement over us getting the land we have been contending for has turned up, but I can tell you that prophetically I can feel we are very close.

Have you felt an increase in warfare recently? Spiritual warfare is a real thing. The Word says:

For our struggle is not against flesh and blood, but against the rulers, against the powers, against the world forces of this darkness, against the spiritual forces of wickedness in the heavenly places (Ephesians 6:12).

Good news is, it's not that you're just having a hard time. No, no! There have been real principalities assigned to blocking you from walking into the fullness of your destiny.

But Jesus!

I don't want to undermine the fact that warfare is real, but we can't place our focus on it. Last time I checked, Jesus crushed satan under His feet: "The God of peace will soon crush Satan under your feet" (Rom. 16:20). So we can be victorious even through warfare!

The second good thing is this. If you have felt the warfare around you (or in you—your thoughts) increase dramatically recently, you are close to your promise.

So now's the time to stand in faith.

You will not be moved, unless by God.

You have heard Him clearly.

It's time to take up the shield of faith (see Eph. 6:16).

In Jesus' name, right now I break off a spirit of confusion that is over you or assigned to you in this season. I pray for the truth and blueprints of Heaven to fall to you now. May God break in with clarity over your thoughts, clarity over your direction, and clarity over your focus. I pray for the shalom peace of Jesus to be over your thoughts, body, and soul right now. We take every thought captive now and surrender them to the mind of Christ. Amen.

5. Catch the Lies

Catch the foxes for us, the little foxes that are ruining the vineyards, while our vineyards are in blossom (Song of Solomon 2:15).

Speaking of taking our thoughts captive, this scripture above is so important because often our biggest battleground with the enemy is in our mind.

Foxes can often be the lies that the enemy whispers as we are contending in faith. The enemy is sneaky. Often he sneaks in the back door, just whispering small thoughts to us. That thought, if not addressed, will begin to fester and eventually poison us with doubt about that promise of God.

Here are a few foxes or whispering lies of the enemy to be aware of that are pretty common when you are contending:

- "I can't…"
- "What if that's not God's best choice?"

- "I won't have enough," or "God won't provide everything I need."
- "What if I heard God wrong?"
- "Others won't support me."
- "I'm not good enough, smart enough, pretty enough, wealthy enough, strong enough" etc.
- "I'll never be free of this."
- "It's my fault I'm stuck."
- "It must be God's will for me to be like this."
- "God won't come through for me."
- "Maybe I should settle for less."
- "If I do this, the warfare will never stop."
- "It's too hard."
- "It's too big of a miracle."
- "It won't ever happen."
- "Maybe the timing is off."

Did you find one you've been struggling with lately?

Take some time and pray this if you have found a lie you've been thinking. You can use this prayer with a different lie if you recognize one that you have really been struggling with.

> *Jesus, I have really been struggling with the lie that _____. In Jesus' name, I renounce my agreement with the lie that _____. I*

*pray and claim the truth that _____ (here
ask the Holy Spirit to reveal truth to you). Amen.*

Whatever that truth is that the Holy Spirit revealed, I want to encourage you to write it out like a scripture and paste it up where you can see it—on your mirror, on your computer screen, in your car, maybe even on a sticky note on the inside of your shoes (done that before!).

You need the truth of God surrounding yourself in this moment to keep you on track, to keep you focused, and to extinguish the enemy's fiery arrows of doubt.

Found within the footnotes of *The Passion Translation* for Song of Solomon 2:15 it says:

> These "foxes" are the compromises that are hidden deep in our hearts. These are areas of our lives where we have not yet allowed the victory of Christ to shine. The foxes keep the fruit of his Spirit from growing within us.

What gets compromised the most as we are contending for a promise of God is our faith.

So, can I challenge you with a question?

How's your faith today?

Has your faith been under attack?

What's the one truth you are reclaiming today and decreeing over your situation?

6. Strengthen Your Net—Gather Your Intercessors

Perhaps you are one of the people reading this right now who already has a wild dream that the Holy Spirit planted in you. You are a pioneer, and you are standing in faith for something way bigger than anything you could do on your own. Can I give you a tip from one pioneer to another? Gather some other faith-filled friends to petition Heaven with you for your promise.

As pioneers, we tend to be driven, sometimes can be narrow focused, and independent also. Can I get a hallelujah right there! That's right! I'm talking to you! And me too!

A while back, I learned how it is so important that you bring people into the dream God has placed on you and ask them to pray alongside. I am convinced that much unnecessary warfare us frontline leaders go through often is because our net of intercessors who hold us up is weak.

When I was first stepping out in ministry, the warfare we would go through as a family was unreal. Before trips, I would kind of casually ask friends to pray. When I started to learn the power of having coverage with intercessors who would stand alongside me in prayer, I stopped being casual about asking for prayer.

Prayer unlocks things from Heaven. It's important that you gather people around your calling, your vision, your purpose and ask them to pray—even if it's just one person. When I say pray, I don't mean just the casual response, "Yeah, I'll pray for you," but then they don't actually pray. I mean people who, when asked to pray for you, will storm Heaven in intercession and declare into the situation using the Word as their sword. There have been many times I have relied on my intercessors, as I send them an SOS email or text saying, "Pray now!"

Once I got a better support net of intercessors holding up my ministry with their prayers, guess what? Way less warfare!

Prayer works!

It's time to pray the prayers that release the response from Heaven.

Here are a few scriptures I recommend your intercessors pray over you and into the promise of God:

> *I will place on his shoulder the key to the house of David; what he opens no one can shut, and what he shuts no one can open* (Isaiah 22:22 NIV).

> *The Lord will make you the head, not the tail. If you pay attention to the commands of the Lord your God that I give you this day and carefully follow them, you will always be at the top, never at the bottom* (Deuteronomy 28:13 NIV).

I pray that out of his glorious riches he may strengthen you with power through his Spirit in your inner being (Ephesians 3:16 NIV).

Also read the whole chapter of Psalm 91.

7. Get Wisdom

Make your ear attentive to wisdom; incline your heart to understanding. For if you cry out for insight, and raise your voice for understanding; if you seek her as silver and search for her as for hidden treasures; then you will understand the fear of the Lord, and discover the knowledge of God. For the Lord gives wisdom; from His mouth come knowledge and understanding. He stores up sound wisdom for the upright; He is a shield to those who walk in integrity (Proverbs 2:2-7).

In Gibeon the Lord appeared to Solomon in a dream at night; and God said, "Ask what you wish Me to give you."

…[Then Solomon said,] "So give Your servant an understanding heart to judge Your people, to discern between good and evil" (1 Kings 3:5,9).

Wisdom is such a key for us pioneers. I know I keep writing to the pioneers, but as I was praying about this book I felt like many, many pioneers would be the ones reading through these pages.

As you step into the new or are contending for breakthrough, in the midst of all that contending, it's so important to step back and ask for wisdom. It's often hard for us to take a step back, especially if we have been contending for so long. Someone might come along who shares an opinion, and the fleshly temptation can sometimes be to respond proudly, "Well, I've tried that before and it didn't work," or, "I've thought of that, but…" etc.

King Solomon was given the golden question I think all of us would want. Imagine God Himself comes up to you today and says, "Ask Me for what you want." What would you say?

Because he asked for wisdom, Solomon had favor!

I remember many years ago sitting across the table from Patricia King, my spiritual mom. I shared with her our vision from the Lord and the word Sam and I had heard that we would be moving to build a place of respite.

"Where do you think it is?" she asked.

I told her that I had wondered if it was moving back to Redding, California—the place we had lived during our first year of marriage. Excitedly, I shared with her, "I'm going this fall to visit it with my assistant and just put my feet on the land and see what God has to say."

"Hmm," she pondered for a second. "I don't think you will find the same grace for there as when you were first there," she replied.

Ouch! Not the response I was hoping to hear. But you know what? She was right! She had heard from the Lord accurately and spoken wisely.

On a side note, I loved my time back visiting Redding, and I still love the special place Bethel church has in our hearts—but it just wasn't the same. As I walked the property, I heard the Holy Spirit's clear direction: "This will be a place where you come to refresh, but not where I'm moving you to."

It's not always easy to hear alternate opinions outside of the one in your head, but it's so necessary.

I advise you, think of someone in your life. Someone who knows you well, wants what's best for you, and is willing to give you an honest opinion. Take them out to lunch and really explain to them the promise of God you are contending for. Ask them to pray and seek the Lord for you and provide you with wisdom if they hear anything.

On the flip side, as you are standing in faith, be careful who you listen to for wisdom. Make sure they are not operating out of fear or control, but really, truly are seeking the Lord for you. Make sure they are full of faith and also are not afraid to offend you with truth. That's wisdom!

8. No Compromise

When you have heard a clear word from God, you must not compromise.

DO NOT COMPROMISE.

I remember just a few months ago when I was ministering at Joan Hunter's church. Now, no one knew it in the room, but during worship I was talking to and hearing from the Lord about our future land. I was reminding God of His promise for us, and He was speaking back to me.

In the middle of me being lost in this transaction with the Lord, someone from the stage started saying something about compromise. Startled in my thoughts and conversation with God, I remember clearly the statement being released: "Do not settle! I repeat, do not settle!" The fire of God hit me, and I knew the Lord was trumpeting that message.

The Lord gave a wonderful promise to Moses and the people of Israel—the Promised Land, the land flowing with milk and honey. When they were to cross over the Jordan, though, there was a very specific instruction from the Lord.

> *Then the Lord spoke to Moses in the plains of Moab by the Jordan opposite Jericho, saying, "Speak to the sons of Israel and say to them,*

> 'When you cross the Jordan into the land of Canaan, you shall drive out all the inhabitants of the land from you, and destroy all their idolatrous sculptures, destroy all their cast metal images, and eliminate all their high places; and you shall take possession of the land and live in it, for I have given the land to you to possess it'" (Numbers 33:50-53).

So there was the command—drive out all of the inhabitants in the land. God also gave them a warning if they did not do this.

> But if you do not drive out the inhabitants of the land from you, then it will come about that those whom you let remain of them will be like thorns in your eyes and like pricks in your sides, and they will trouble you in the land in which you live. And just as I plan to do to them, I will do to you (Numbers 33:55-56).

It's a pretty clear warning. If you do not drive out all the people in the land, when you go in and conquer it, it will bring you trouble in the end.

Now if you fast-forward in the Bible to the book of Joshua, something very interesting happened with the Gibeonites and the Israelites that's worth reading and thinking over.

When Joshua and the Israelites began conquering land, the Gibeonites got very crafty or sneaky and disguised themselves as poor outsiders just traveling through. They asked Joshua and the Israelites to make a covenant oath with them. And guess what happened?

> *It came about at the end of three days after they had made a covenant with them, that they heard that they were neighbors and that they were living within their land* (Joshua 9:16).

Joshua and the Israelites compromised the instructions they were told. Instead of conquering the Gibeonites, they allowed them to stay living there in their promised land. Yes, the Israelites were deceived and lied to, but they did not follow through with what God had told them to do. They compromised.

And guess what happened? Later five kings came to attack the people of Gibeon, and Joshua and the Israelites had to fight on their behalf because of that oath. Bottom line—Joshua and the Israelites had to go to war against something they were never meant to (see Josh. 10).

Hello! Did you read that?

When you and I compromise and settle for less than what God has promised, we can end up having more troubles in the end than if we had just trusted God to begin with. We end up drawing unnecessary battles to ourselves.

So do not settle. In the process of waiting for that promise to come, as you contend in faith and stand on what God has spoken, do not settle for less.

It's important, in this moment, for us to take a moment and revisit the original word the Lord spoke to you and me about our promises. What are the prophetic words that have been spoken to you by the Lord or by others?

As a parabolic prophet (one who often lives out the message God is speaking to the church), I'm declaring this very message over myself now! Do not settle or compromise!

Sometimes in that process of waiting—or if our promise from God seems so far-fetched or, dare I say the "I" word (impossible)—the temptation arises to settle for something that may be similar to the promise but a little less than God's best. Also, a misguided word from an outsider may come along to pull you off target while you're waiting. Although it sounds similar to what God shared with you, it isn't quite 100 percent the word; it's not what God said. Someone just got a revelation while reading that! Hallelujah!

Let's believe God today for His very best. Let's believe that the word He gave us hasn't changed and isn't less than what He said. Let's dare to just believe God for His word.

Hiccups and Discouragement

You know, this book would not be complete without adding this section. It's an honest, heartfelt section that I hope will encourage you in whatever stage of the process of walking into your promise you find yourself today.

"So when are you guys going to move? When is your promised land coming?" a friend asked me out loud at a prophetic meeting in front of a large group of people.

"Soon!" I smiled back and responded. (Inwardly, I struggled.) I had figured out the best response to people who would ask—well-meaning friends who were all believing in the promise for us. This wasn't the first time I had been asked, so I had figured out the best response.

However, if I were honest, the constant asking every time we got together was grinding my assured faith down. I knew our friends were all excited for us and praying, but I wished I could have a real answer with a timeline for them. The truth is, even as I am writing this now, I still don't.

Believing, yes.

Trusting, yes

Weary in the process—honest truth—yes!

Then suddenly one day, we got momentum. A contact I had met at an event reached out to Sam and me with hope.

"I'd like to help you. I'd like to have my attorney look into the property you guys are looking at," she said, and reminded me, "Don't you know who your Daddy is!"

"DON'T YOU KNOW WHO YOUR DADDY IS!"

That confident phrase is something I will keep reminding myself probably for the rest of my life!

Her faith was challenging mine for the better. I always thought of myself as pretty faith filled. I've seen hundreds if not thousands of miracles of God, but still I am being challenged in this area.

We had found a piece of property, one we loved and thought fit perfectly the words and vision God had given us. With hope in our spirits, we planned a family vacation to all go walk the land. Putting my own feet in the next place God is calling me has always been something I have to do with the Lord and allow Him to confirm.

We fell in love with the land, the possibility the land held. Returning home, Sam and I started dreaming with God. We printed out the latitude and longitude coordinates of it, and started envisioning where we would put our own family house; where a big worship barn would go; where the respite house for prophets, apostles, and ministry leaders would be on the property; where the hiking trails and places of encounter would be to meet with Jesus. It was a big vision, but we were riding high in the sky with excitement.

And then, one morning, it started with just a feeling. Call it doubt, or maybe even a hunch. I started to hear a daunting question inside my head: *But what if it's not this land?*

Trying to push the question aside, I still refused to lay down my dream for the land. I rebuked the enemy, who I believed to be the one speaking. (Hopefully I'm not the only one who does this here.) We had posted the pictures up in our office, so in my daily time of prayer I'd put my hands on those pictures and declare that the Lord would do exceedingly above and beyond our wildest dreams! I also prayed that the Lord would shut any door that isn't His to walk through and open the right ones, according to Isaiah 22:22:

> *Then I will put the key of the house of David on his shoulder; when he opens, no one will shut, when he shuts, no one will open.*

So we started making phone calls, one after another, trying to reach the county offices to see if all that we wanted to do with the land was legally allowed. Person after person sent us to call someone else; that someone else would, of course, not pick up or not return our phone call.

Finally, one early morning before the kids woke up, my eyes laid hold of the email I had been waiting for.

The subject bar read "Regarding the Land" and was from the county official. A sinking feeling came to my stomach. That same feeling I had once had, which I so quickly brushed aside, had returned.

I opened the email.

"Regarding the land with the coordinates you have sent us, I have some not so good news. The land is protected by the county law, and is not able to be divided and not truly fitting the vision you have to do with it. I would not be able to sign off on your vision for it."

Here came what I like to call the hiccup or bump in the road. And just so you know, by the way, we aren't past this hiccup right now. Nope. Some people like to share stories only after they have attained their victory, but this is fresh off the press. As I'm writing it, I'm going through it with you.

Sad, yes.

Grieved, yes.

Totally discouraged, never!

> ## AT SOME POINT ALL OF US HAVE TO FACE A MOMENT WHEN WE HAVE TO READJUST, PERHAPS TAKE A STEP BACK, AND REEVALUATE.

I am convinced that at some point all of us have to face a moment when we have to readjust, perhaps take a step back, and reevaluate. Do you find yourself at that place today?

It's a time to say—will I still stand strong in faith, even as a storm hits? Even when the slam of a closed door comes stinging to my face, will I still believe in His promise?

So I found myself digging down deep and asking myself the question, "Well, what really were the words the Lord has spoken to us? Did I misinterpret any of those words or stretch them to make them fit my mold of what I thought He was saying?"

> ## I STILL BELIEVE, I WON'T GIVE UP, AND I WON'T QUIT.

Good, honest questions.

Following that, my conversation with Jesus went something like this—I prayed:

Lord, help me to see clearly. I bring my disappointment with this process before You. It's been a long time, Lord, and a lot of research. It's been a long trial of trusting You when all looked bleak.

God, I don't know why I do, but I still believe. I believe You are still good, even though this feels like a totally shut door. I still believe in the promise and I believe it's coming soon for some reason. I believe You are clear and not misguiding.

You don't change. I know You are the one who has laid this vision out for me to do, so please come and bring clarity. Where have I heard wrong or interpreted wrong, God? It's always so easy for me to hear clearly for others, but for my own self it's challenging. God, I doubt my own ability to even hear clearly for myself in this moment. I need Your help, Lord. I pray for the fog to lift so I can see the clear, peaceful path that's Heaven's choice here.

I refuse to believe this time spent was wasted. Through it You have taught me so much about trusting and standing in faith. My faith muscles have increased. My boldness to step into new territory has grown. I won't let the enemy make me look back now in discouragement and defeat. Lord, show me the path forward. God, will You catch me in this moment that feels like a setback?

I still believe. I won't give up, and I won't quit. Amen.

He Works Everything for Good

If you are like me and finding yourself in a hiccup or bump in the road right now, the honest truth is I don't have answers for you.

But I do have Jesus. He's all I know to fall back on right now, and He's all you've got when you're facing this storm of discouragement.

Romans 8:28 says God works everything for good according to His purpose, and I truly do believe that. I may not understand His timing or His ways, but I do trust Him in everything—even the valleys.

My disappointments are not a reflection of His love or His character. I know this process is developing me. My faith muscles are being stretched, and I know yours are too! Are we going to really believe today that His word still remains, that the promise is still there? When I read history books of great faith leaders, what often gets overlooked is the process those leaders went through, those valleys they walked through where their faith and love for Jesus were put on trial, which developed the character that they now carry.

You are in process! You are being developed! Hallelujah! Our faith muscles are increasing today. You are being promoted to a new level of faith!

Let's take a moment and do the absolute opposite of what the enemy of this world would want us to do. Let's thank God. Let's overcome this valley or this moment of disappointment through the weapon of praise.

Jehoshaphat sent the worshipers out first on the battlefield (see 2 Chron. 20:21). Why would he ever want to injure his worship team, you might ask? Because he knew something. He knew that the power of praise and thanksgiving is what defeats the enemy when we are in the thickest moment of warfare. And by the way, overcoming disappointment is a time of war!

So let's take a moment to enter His gates through our thanksgiving. Pray with me:

Thank You, Jesus, for this trial today. Lord, I praise You for You are good no matter what. Thank You, Lord, that Your word in Jeremiah 29:11 says that You have a plan and a purpose for my life, plans to prosper me and not to harm me, plans to give me a hope and a future. Thank You, God, that You are sovereign. You know the direction and path for my life and ministry. You know what lies ahead for my family. I praise You, Jesus, that You are in control. I thank You, God, that I can hear You clearly. And I thank You, Lord, that You still have a promise for my life, although it might look different than what I expected in this season. You still have a plan and it is good! Thank You, Jesus! I declare now that Your blood is still enough to redeem me, to cleanse me, to set me free. I thank You, Lord, that this place is not my eternal home, but just a place in passing. I thank You that I can set my eyes on You, Jesus, and You will help me rise above this valley of disappointment now. Hallelujah! I may not see the whole picture, but I thank You, Lord, that You are giving me the next step. Thank You for this moment to build my faith. My heart rejoices in the One I love. Your love is more than enough to sustain me and renew me. Hallelujah! Amen.

CHAPTER 7

Rest Is Faith!

I know what you are thinking—faith and rest don't seem to go hand in hand! Boy, was I surprised one day when the Lord talked to me about rest.

To give a backdrop for where we were in contending for our promise of God, we had been believing for that land that the Lord had first showed me for over six years now. I had stood on the word of God, fasted, and prayed countless hours. I had shared the vision with a few faith-filled friends and asked for wisdom and prayers. We had drawn our vision up on the wall, laid hands on it, and declared that God is faithful. I had thought every which way around it that you can think of, and wondered what else I needed to be doing. Even our young kids got involved and prayed with us often in the evenings before bed for our "farm from God" (in my daughter's words).

And then one day, He spoke something that surprised me a little. It was early morning, before the rest of the house was up, which is always my best time with the Lord, I might add.

I could feel His Presence in the room right as I walked in. "Lord. I know You're near. I can feel You. What's on Your heart, Abba?" I whispered in prayer.

And then, I heard His voice: "Ana, I want to show you something," He said. And just like that, I was taken into a vision with the Lord.

I saw myself and Jesus sitting in an open boat similar to a large canoe. We rode out together on a crystal clear lake. Stillness. I dared not say anything because the Presence of God was so thick, and I wanted to not miss anything He might say.

Finally, after what felt like hours but was really in retrospect only ten minutes of staring out to the horizon of that lake, Jesus spoke to me. He looked at me with a smile and a twinkling of joy in His eyes. "Ana, right now the best thing you can do is just rest. Rest for you is faith."

And just like that, I was back in my office, no longer seeing Jesus, but His Presence stayed lingering. *Rest?* I pondered out loud. *What does that even look like?*

Yet those who wait for the Lord will gain new strength; they will mount up with wings like eagles, they will run and not get tired, they will walk and not become weary (Isaiah 40:31).

Then I turned to this scripture in my Bible, and the words seemed to jump off the page at me, as they are for you right now, probably! Thank You, Holy Spirit! The imagery of mounting up with wings like eagles caused me to pause.

Eagles don't beat their wings frantically trying to find their balance. They majestically outstretch their wings, find the right wind, and glide across the sky peacefully. Eagles also have laser vision that targets their prey when they see it.

We pioneers tend to be go-getters. Those of us who have had to contend and stand on our promise for quite some time often struggle with moving in faith from the place of rest. We can get so caught in the pattern or doing, pushing, pressing in faith that we forget what Jesus taught us about rest.

So do not worry about tomorrow; for tomorrow will worry about itself. Each day has enough trouble of its own (Matthew 6:34).

Now on one of those days Jesus and His disciples got into a boat, and He said to them, "Let's cross over to the other side of the lake." So they launched out. But as they were sailing along He fell asleep; and a fierce gale of wind descended on the lake, and they began to be swamped and to be in danger. They came up to Jesus and woke Him, saying, "Master, Master, we are perishing!" And He got up and rebuked the wind and the surging waves, and they stopped, and it became calm. And He said to them, "Where is your faith?" But they were fearful and amazed, saying to one another, "Who then is this, that He commands even the winds and the water, and they obey Him?" (Luke 8:22-25).

I'm going to be bold here and just say it. Some of us need to let go of the pursuit of our promise for a season, if He calls us to it, and just rest in trust.

> ## SOME OF US NEED TO LET GO OF THE PURSUIT OF OUR PROMISE FOR A SEASON, IF HE CALLS US TO IT, AND JUST REST IN TRUST.

Yes, there is a season to run! Yes, there is a season to push and press! Yes, there is a season to stand in faith. But you know what's the hardest for us pioneers? The season when God asks us to lay it down and just simply rest.

The next morning I was meditating on that scripture and was processing what the Lord had said. "Okay,

God, what does rest even look like? I've been standing in faith and contending for so long!" Just then I received a text from Patricia King. (Patricia does text me, often just at the right moment when I need it the most. I'm so grateful for my spiritual momma and the impact she has made for the Kingdom!)

Her text leapt out at me from my phone there in the wee hours of the morning. "Do you feel like you are supposed to perhaps take a season of rest from the pursuit of the land? I just feel the promise still remains, but that maybe God's asking you to rest from it, take a step back, and get some perspective."

I literally laughed out loud! Boy, does God know me. He knows and understands your very makeup too! I know that it's not by mistake that you picked up this book. You have been contending and believing for so long for your promise of God. No doubt, you have had to push past discouragement and past moments when you felt like giving up. So I know that this idea of taking a step back and resting from the push and drive of contending might seem as contrary to you right now as it did for me that early morning when I received that text.

Then the Lord took me into a heavenly vision. I found myself in a courtroom. There were many different seats there, and I saw many other people besides me there in the room. My name was called out, and I was asked to step forward and state my case.

As I stood up, I felt the fear of the Lord come over me. I saw a very large seat in the center of the other seats, and saw a white light radiating off of it. In the moment, I knew this was my chance before the Father to state my case over the land.

I spoke up.

"Thank You for allowing me this chance to stand before You and the others here in this courtroom. I come before You today to ask about the land You have promised us. God, I ask You, where is it? Why hasn't the promise manifested yet? You have shown me it in countless visions. I have walked the land with You, Jesus, hand in hand. You have spoken to me about the provision that would be granted to me to acquire the land, and as well the blessings for generations from the land. I have interceded, declared Your word, and stood in faith. Have I done something wrong? Why is there delay?"

Then a moment happened that still brings me to tears even now as I type this.

He stood up.

I couldn't see the face of the Father, but I saw His robes. A booming voice responded back to me. "Ana, you have mistaken My process as delay. I am preparing your blessing."

Boy, did that heavenly experience in the courtroom instantly change my perspective on "process."[1] Do you believe that today? God is preparing your blessing.

Sometimes God has to nearly beat us over the head to get us stubborn ones to obey what we are hearing! (Oh boy, as I write this I can just see the emails rolling in from people's misunderstandings! Just to clarify, God is a loving God. He is gentle, He is kind, He is wise. Sometimes He does have to nearly scream at us, reconfirming things over and over, until we finally go, "Huh, maybe God's trying to say something to me. Maybe I should change my ways and obey!")

> **"YOU HAVE MISTAKEN MY PROCESS AS DELAY. I AM PREPARING YOUR BLESSING."**

So could God be asking you to take a break from the contending and rest for a season? He's not asking you to give up. It's quite the opposite. He's calling you to the very place of rest Jesus Himself was in as the disciples faced the storm. Everything may look bleak right now, or perhaps even stormy, but God has said it—so it shall be.

But how? You might ask! (I know, because I said the same thing to God that morning!) Guess what? I asked Him, and boy, was I surprised when He responded.

"Stop looking for the land. Stop hunting through Zillow and other real estate websites trying to find where this promised land is. For a season, Ana, you are not to even look." Then He added, because He knows me so well, "And every time you feel tempted to look, shut your computer off and say out loud: 'I trust you that it's coming and I believe.'"

It's as if He knew, because boy, was that a challenge for me. Luckily, I have good, close friends who reminded me, "But didn't God say to rest from the pursuit of the land right now?"

So I want you to take a moment with the Holy Spirit. Ask Him, "God, are You challenging me for a season to take a step back from the pursuit of this? And is there something practical I need to do that can help me rest?"

Pray this with me:

> *God, I surrender my pursuit of this today. Lord, I want Your timing and Your peace. I want Your best and Your blessing over this promise. I'm not quitting, but I am choosing to stop pushing so hard to make things happen on my own. God, I chose to lay down in rest now. Thank You that You are giving me this opportunity to stretch, to grow, to trust You at another level. Amen.*

Note

1. As a side note, my friend Robert Henderson teaches on the courts of Heaven. He backs this up with biblical explanation. If you are curious

150

and want to know more about operating in the courts of Heaven, I suggest you check out his website, roberthenderson.org, where you can get all his materials.

CHAPTER 8

Go Occupy! It's Time to Take the Land

As I prayed about the title of this book, the Lord clearly spoke to me. I saw a picture of many people charging up what looked like a giant mountain. I could see a spirit of defeat following closely behind them, and they tiredly wanted to give up. "Don't give up!" I wanted to yell out. "You're so close to the promise!" With nothing but rugged mountain terrain in their eyesight, little did the people realize just how close they were to crossing over.

Now is the time! If I could be a coach running right behind you right now, I would yell, "Don't quit! You're right there!"

Little do you realize how close you are!

When I felt like giving up on the respite center vision the Lord had given me, suddenly I saw a bridge being built. It's been my experience that often we are waiting for the promise of God to descend upon us like a giant cupcake that falls in our lap. (Sorry, I'm hungry right now and it was the image that came to mind!)

But often, the promise is within reach. Let me explain better. We are often looking for God to do a miracle for us, but rather He wants to do a miracle with us. There are tools He will put in your path that will help you climb that mountain, and the tools very well could be bridges or other people who come alongside your vision and help the promise come into fruition.

So I want you to do yourself a favor. Sit back and ask, "What has God already shown me, and who are the people He has put in my path? Are there any steps He has already shown me to take?"

Make Adjustments As God Leads

One more thing I have to add to this book that was such a key for us in attaining our promise is: Do not compromise, but be willing to adjust.

DO NOT COMPROMISE, BUT BE WILLING TO ADJUST.

As the Word says, "We know in part" (see 1 Cor. 13:9). God will show us a vision, and then we may think we understand the full picture when actually we are only seeing a portion of it. The word and promise is still the same yes, but be willing to adjust how you get there if God leads you.

Along our own journey of looking for this piece of property, we thought we knew where the location would be specifically. Then one day, as I was on my knees before the Lord, I heard Him say clearly, "Are you willing to give it up? Are you willing to adjust?"

Six years of contending, believing, and standing when others came to me with their concerns, fighting past discouragement at times, and now God was asking me to give everything up!

Warning: He may ask you the same thing.

Next I flipped open my Bible to a story that helped me process this moment with Jesus.

Some time later God tested Abraham. He said to him, "Abraham!"

"Here I am," he replied.

Then God said, "Take your son, your only son, whom you love—Isaac—and go to the region of Moriah. Sacrifice him there as a burnt offering on a mountain I will show you."

Early the next morning Abraham got up and loaded his donkey. He took with him two of his servants and his son Isaac. When he had cut enough wood for the burnt offering, he set out for the place God had told him about. On the third day Abraham looked up and saw the place in the distance. He said to his servants, "Stay here with the donkey while I and the boy go over there. We will worship and then we will come back to you."

Abraham took the wood for the burnt offering and placed it on his son Isaac, and he himself carried the fire and the knife. As the two of them went on together, Isaac spoke up and said to his father Abraham, "Father?"

"Yes, my son?" Abraham replied.

"The fire and wood are here," Isaac said, "but where is the lamb for the burnt offering?"

Abraham answered, "God himself will provide the lamb for the burnt offering, my son." And the two of them went on together.

When they reached the place God had told him about, Abraham built an altar there and arranged the wood on it. He bound his son Isaac and laid him on the altar, on top of the wood. Then he reached out his hand and took the knife to slay his son. But the angel of the Lord called out to him from heaven, "Abraham! Abraham!"

"Here I am," he replied.

"Do not lay a hand on the boy," he said. "Do not do anything to him. Now I know that you fear God, because you have not withheld from me your son, your only son."

Abraham looked up and there in a thicket he saw a ram caught by its horns. He went over and took the ram and sacrificed it as a burnt offering instead of his son. So Abraham called that place The Lord Will Provide. And to this day it is said, "On the mountain of the Lord it will be provided" (Genesis 22:1-14 NIV).

At the end of the day, Abraham passed that test of faith. As hard as it is to understand why a loving God would ask him to do that—give up the very promise God had given him in the first place—there was a test: "Do you love the promise more than you love Me? If I ask you, would you be willing to lay it all down?"

With tears streaming down my face, I prayed:

God, I surrender it all. I don't know why You are asking this, but Lord, if You have other plans now for my family, then I want to be in the center of Your plans and not my own. Your plans are better than my own. I may not understand, but I will trust You. I still love You.

And then the voice came again: "The promise still remains, but are you willing to adjust?"

Can I take a moment here and prophesy to you? We are in a season of flexibility. God is asking many of us to build, but in the building process we have to be willing to lay it all down, surrender our own plans, to pick it back up again with the assignment from Heaven. In our surrender, He knows He can trust us with more. The promise of God has to be laid down, given back to Him, and fully surrendered so that the promise doesn't become an idol above our relationship with Jesus. I found that after my own process of surrender, then the momentum came.

AFTER THE SURRENDER, THEN MOMENTUM COMES.

Sometimes, because we lack the full vision and perspective that God has, we might think, *This is the only way I am going to get to that promise.* Then along the journey of climbing that mountain, God may hand you a hot-air balloon and say, "I have a different route for you to get to the top. Will you trust Me?"

So Jesus asked me, "Are you willing to adjust?" and I took that question seriously. It was really more of a command than a question. We have free will, of course, but at the end of the day, if Jesus asks me, "Are you willing to…" I am always going to say yes!

Next I found myself in a vision with the Lord. He still speaks in visions and gives revelation through visions sometimes. Just look at how He spoke to John in the book of Revelation! Always test everything you see with the Word of God, of course. Does what you are seeing match the nature of Christ you read about in the Bible?

In the vision, Jesus took me to a large room in Heaven—one I have seen before. He then unrolled a scroll and said, "I want to show you a few more details about your land." Looking over His shoulder, I viewed tall, pointy trees. Then He smiled and drew with His finger a winding blue line through the middle of the paper. "Look for the winding creek," He said.

I came out of that vision, and I knew something had been opened in Heaven. Something that had previously felt locked had now been opened by my willingness to surrender it all. Clarity was starting to flow. Sam and I took that word, "Are you willing to adjust?" and really listened to it. Long story short, the Holy Spirit took us on a wonderful treasure hunt of mapping out all the prophetic words and details the Lord had shared with us over the years, piecing them all together, letting go of our previous expectations of where the land could be, and suddenly God did it.

God did a suddenly!

Up popped our exact promised land for a place of respite for prophets, apostles, and ministry leaders! A large piece of property came up for sale at just that moment. It had golden yellow fields I had seen in visions for years; lined with tall, pointy trees; and, get this, a small winding creek running through the very center of the land.

God was preparing it all along. Or perhaps, just perhaps, He was preparing us through the process.

HE WAS PREPARING US THROUGH THE PROCESS.

Do not compromise but be willing to adjust as God leads. This is a key now for you and crossing over. You're right there at the pinnacle.

Adjust to what the voice of God is telling you. Lay down your own agenda, or even what you thought the plan was. The promise is still there, it just may look different than what you expected, or even how you expected to get there. God is releasing the blueprints to you now.

With faith and trust as your step by step, I have no doubt you will get there.

Now is the time! Go take the land!

Be bold and courageous.

> *For you are about to cross the Jordan to go in to take possession of the land which the Lord your God is giving you, and you shall possess it and live in it* (Deuteronomy 11:31).

About the Author

Ana Werner and her husband, Sam, reside in Missouri with their two beautiful children. She is the founder of Eaglets Network and Ana Werner Ministries. Ana travels internationally and equips people to see in the Spirit, move in the prophetic, and experience healing and deliverance through her ministry. Her transparency as she shares the realities and experiences she has had in Heaven brings the Holy Spirit, the love of the Father, and the power of God into the room when she speaks. Ana is passionate about leading people into encountering Jesus' heart.

For more about Ana's ministry and mentorships, visit anawerner.org.